The Outsiders

John Pilger
and Michael Coren

The Outsiders

Quartet Books
London Melbourne New York
in association with
Channel Four Television Company Limited

First published by Quartet Books Limited 1985
A member of the Namara Group
27/29 Goodge Street, London WIP IFD

British Library Cataloguing in Publication Data

Pilger, John
    The outsiders.
    1. Great Britain—Politics and government
    —1979–
    I. Title   II. Coren, Michael
    320.941   JN231

    ISBN 0-7043-2489-X

Typeset by MC Typeset, Chatham, Kent
Printed and bound in Great Britain
by Mackays of Chatham Ltd, Kent

From John, to Yvonne and Sam.

From Mike, to his parents.

Contents

Acknowledgements

During 1981 John Pilger interviewed nine people in a Channel 4 television series entitled 'The Outsiders'. Michael Coren was the researcher on seven of these programmes. This book is a collection of those interviews, cut and edited accordingly, with introductions to provide factual background. One extra chapter, on Ken Livingstone, has been included; this interview took place separately from the series.

The authors would like to thank the following people for their help: Jacky Stoller (producer), Alan Lowery (director), Timothy O'Grady, Hugh Munro, Ping Mudie, everybody at Tempest Films and all the crews who worked on the programmes. To the people who kindly gave up scarce and valuable time to be quoted in the introductions we owe a debt of gratitude; and of course to the ten men and women here interviewed. The photographs are all reproduced by courtesy of Tempest Films and Glen Ratcliffe, except that of Ken Livingstone, reproduced by courtesy of the Greater London Council, and that of Wilfred Burchett, by Bill Ray.

Introduction

What is an outsider? There is no easy answer to this question, as all of us involved in the production of the series came to realize after considering not only those people we had rejected, but also those we had chosen. Over a period of one year we eliminated a large number of people who, initially, had seemed eligible. They ranged from businessmen and actresses, to sportsmen and retired criminals. We approached everyone by letter, in which we posed our working definition of 'outsider': 'People who for significant periods during distinguished lives have been outside the establishment, and whose talent places them beyond labels and institutions.' We asked Sean MacBride, our first outsider, to give his definition. 'Somebody', he said, 'who is able to influence thinking and actions of people without being actually in charge of a government or part of an establishment.' Although they sounded satisfactory, neither definition was appropriate for Ken Livingstone, so obviously an outsider and yet, at the time of writing, leader of one of the world's larger units of government: the Greater London Council.

If wealth, power, success or privilege disqualified someone from being an outsider, several of those we have chosen would have been ineligible. Clearly it was more pragmatic to be arbitrary in our choices, and gauge the suitability of each person according to broader criteria. In doing so we were able to make a distinctive and varied selection, far more revealing than one based on some specific and narrower definition. Some individuals were outsiders by choice, others by necessity. Some had made the choice out of discontent with an existing state of affairs, hoping to remedy the situation through words, actions and, not least, artistic endeavour.

Salman Rushdie was privately educated, and is both eminently successful and financially secure. But this is of little interest to some people in certain parts of the inner city where, because of his skin colour, he is as likely to be humiliated and even physically attacked as is a sweat-shop worker from Stepney. Wilfred Burchett epitomized the integrity and courage of the outsider. He could easily have slipped into the role of successful and respected media worker, but chose a life which brought him much pain and anguish. He was threatened, abused, and at one period even made stateless. As a man on the Left, he would often identify with a cause, but disillusionment prevented him from staying 'inside' any regime or country for too long.

A telling example of someone born into a ruling class from which few chose to escape is Jessica Mitford. She decided to break the rules, ignore the accepted way of life, and leave her family and country in order to support the revolutionary Left and commit herself to radical politics. There could be no casual falling back into privilege for someone so uncharacteristically principled as Jessica Mitford. Threatened by governments and mob violence, she has nevertheless survived and continues to work for those ideals which inspired her as a young woman.

As a young Australian, David Williamson represents a nation whose people have been considered outsiders for a long time: comrades in times of trouble, colonials and ex-criminals otherwise. Williamson represents the new independent spirit of Australia, and in his plays and politics he explores this growing sense of individuality and character. In a similar way, Martha Gellhorn's challenging journalism offers a critical reappraisal of old ideals, and is very much a part of the American radical tradition. As a woman in the male-dominated world of war reporting, she occupies a unique and once unimaginable position.

Helen Suzman lays easy claim to being an outsider. A female, Jewish liberal living in the South Africa of suspicion and intolerance, she was a lone voice for many years. She will never be accepted by that society, just as she will never accept its values. Greek-born Costa Gavras has spent all his working life questioning governments and elites. As a film director he is experienced in the art of looking in from the outside, showing things in a new light and from an odd angle. It is not only a matter of professional skill, in that his technical viewpoint is somehow appropriate to his critical stance. He is also an outsider in terms of the film industry, continuing to make 'political' films for a mass audience.

Any worries we may have had about dealing with establishment figures proved unfounded when we came to the two we had chosen. Sean MacBride was on the British army's 'wanted' list. Constantly rejecting the chance to spend his time in comfortable positions of authority, he now leads and speaks for organizations whose sole purpose is to help and support outsiders, whether they be political prisoners or people opposing the support of nuclear arms. Ken Livingstone is possibly unique in being a politician who has led the largest unit of local government in Western Europe, yet remained a figure strongly disliked by others with authority and in power. Our idea of the modern politician will certainly have to change in the light of his influence.

It is difficult to express the particular moods and emotions which made these interviews so memorable. In the case of Patsy Spybey, we were uplifted by her enormous courage in confronting the wasting disease with which she was afflicted. She made us feel optimistic and inadequate, and also deeply annoyed at the stupidity and ignorance of others. At many moments there was laughter, as with Jessica Mitford; at others there was sadness and anger, as with Martha Gellhorn's description of Dachau.

After the decision to gather the interviews into this book, we learned of Wilfred Burchett's death. It is impossible to forget this man's modesty, his unsureness as to why we should want to interview him, his nervousness on the day of interview. The image of him sitting in the front room of a suburban house and telling us of his remarkable career is unforgettable.

JP MC
June 1984

1   Sean MacBride

Sean MacBride is a remarkable product of a remarkable family. He was born in 1904 in Paris where his parents were political exiles. His mother was the Irish nationalist Maud Gonne, his father John MacBride was executed by the British after the Easter Rising in 1916. He spent his childhood amongst the literary elite of Ireland's political community: W.B. Yeats, who immortalized Sean's father in a poem, taught him and Ezra Pound instructed him in Latin. As a teenager he joined the Irish Volunteers (later the IRA) and was arrested by the British when he was fourteen. As an able and intelligent young man MacBride came to the notice of Michael Collins and became his personal aide, but was later to fight Collins in the bitter civil war which followed the peace treaty with Britain.

During the period between 1934 and 1935 MacBride was made Chief of Staff of the Irish Republican Army, and after Ireland had secured independence he formed his own political party known (in Gaelic) as Clann na Poblachta (Party of the Republic). In 1948 he became Foreign Minister in a coalition government, building and strengthening Ireland's European ties and establishing the state on the diplomatic scene. But he did not remain in Irish governmental politics for long – indeed he is no longer a universally known figure in the country – and decided to extend his ideas and abilities into the international arena.

In 1961 with several other lawyers – he had undergone legal training between spells of active service with the IRA – he founded Amnesty International. From 1973 to 1976 MacBride was Assistant Secretary-General of the United Nations and its commissioners for Namibia. He also chaired a UNESCO committee reporting on communications problems, and in the early 1970s mediated between the IRA and the loyalist paramilitary organizations in Northern Ireland.

He was awarded the Nobel Peace Prize in 1974, sharing the honour with the Japanese Prime Minister Eisaku Sato. The Nobel committee remarked on MacBride's consistent work for international co-operation, praising efforts which were 'central in contributing to peace in our time'. Three years later he was given the Lenin Peace Prize, the only man ever to have been so recognized by both the Western and Eastern bloc countries.

Though physically no longer a strong man, he is still energetic in the work which various groups continue to ask of him. He recently headed an investigation into the Beirut massacres which took him to Israel and Lebanon. He is a poetic, calm figure with a soothing accent composed of French pronunciation and Irish vowel sounds, of whom this apt description was provided by the chairman of the Lenin prize committee: 'A brilliant example of selfless service to noble ideas of peace and progress'.

JP   You had a unique childhood, one which shaped the idealism which you seem to have lived by.

SM   Idealism is difficult to define, I suppose it's the achievement of a certain state of affairs you ought to be able to bring about. And it conforms with what you conceive to be moral. I've never regarded it as unattainable but you do realize at the back of your mind that you may not be able to achieve everything, you have to be satisfied by stages in a direction. But my commitment to world peace, for example, isn't part of idealism; it is more a realization that, unless we can avoid a third world war, humanity is racing towards its own self-destruction. A question of self-preservation of humanity.

My childhood had a lot to do with any moral sense I now have, which is probably inevitable. To a certain extent I was born into a revolutionary situation; my parents were involved as long as I can remember in movements for the liberation of Ireland, and of Egypt and India and so on. Naturally I learned about Ireland as a child and was involved right from the beginning in the tradition of anti-colonialism and the beginning of the conflict of human rights. My first real experience of violence was World War One. We were caught in the South of France when it started. Within a matter of weeks there were train-loads of wounded soldiers arriving and we helped to establish a hospital there. I remember holding dead and half-dead people – it terrified me but I had to steel myself.

Two years later my father was executed. I learnt about it at a school in Paris and I must say they were extremely good about it. They said that the boys' fathers and mothers were being killed all the time fighting for the small nations. My father was fighting for the liberation of his country and he'd died for the freedom of all nations. I felt he'd died a hero. My mother was arrested many times, she was very emotional and had a less cool head than me. Later I joined the IRA, wondering all the time when we could do something useful. Most of the time was very dull, very dreary, patrolling different streets for hours on end and not quite knowing why.

And then we organized ambushes on the military Auxiliaries, the Black and Tans. They passed through our area the whole time, pretty well. I remember a meeting of the battalion staff at headquarters. I was one of the guards outside. The military came with armoured cars and so on, and our job was to give those inside the building time to escape. I was lying down, and said to my colleague that we'd better retreat. I put my hand out and found his head had been blown to pieces, my hands were full of blood and grey matter. I had to arrange the funeral next morning, I watched his family. I may have killed people, I certainly threw grenades and fired machine-guns in the direction of the British forces; but we had much sterner rules with regard to civilians, always giving street vendors and people time to get out of the way.

I'm not a pacifist in the traditional sense. I do think that violence very seldom achieves the objective it's intended to achieve. It's never justified if there are alternative ways of rectifying what is an injustice, not if there is a peaceful way of doing it by political action or words. That's why I disagree with the IRA very much in the actions they're taking in Northern Ireland at the moment. This should be solved by peaceful means, and very often the violence they indulge in is in excess of what they require. In 1920 we had no parliament of our own, no constitution, no protection for human rights; and we never risked the lives of non-combatants.

JP You've often said that the last remaining friction between the British and the Irish peoples is the partition of Ireland. Why is it of such great importance?

SM Ireland has been a national entity since the beginning of time; it's important to get this in a historical perspective. The country had a tradition, a history and a language of its own, and it's traumatic for such a nation to be suddenly partitioned. The overwhelming majority don't want partition and even though one section don't believe that a political solution can be found – hence the IRA – most people have faith in that method of change. The British have made matters worse by, on the one hand, discriminating both politically and economically and on the other, refusing to face up to the problem. They claim that if the Irish were left to settle their own problems they would kill each other. Not at all!

The solution is to impose a deadline, say, two years, when the British will withdraw completely from Northern Ireland. In the meanwhile have a sample of constitutions, settle what the future of the country will be. I think you'll probably emerge with a federal solution giving the North the complete right to write their own constitution, and use could be made of the Council of Europe which is a valuable body accepted in England, Belfast and Dublin. That would provide a safeguard for human rights. With the Commission for Human Rights it's worked very well in Europe, and could investigate complaints and protect the borders in the United Federal Ireland. In ten or twenty years' time there will be a nationalist majority in Northern Ireland; it would be much better to face a solution now with the goodwill of Britain, the Unionists and the people in the south of Ireland.

The IRA and the para-military groups will agree to a federal solution in the end. They're much closer to it than people think and certainly much closer to each other. They very often discuss solutions and at one time agreed that the British should leave; though not agreeing as to what should happen the next day. I don't think you can argue that there would be a bloodbath if the British left; after all, about 3,000 people were killed in the last ten or twelve years. It's the one portion of Europe where there is constant warfare going on. The religious differences have, to an extent, been built up by the British government; it suits the British parties there to provoke certain sectarian acts in the North. There have been some quite impressive revelations recently on that.

JP You have said that 'there's been a change in the centre of gravity of power from governments to public opinion'.

What did you mean by that?

SM   Remember democracy is a terribly new concept in our world. The
idea of demolition of colonialism and human rights is also new.
Human rights were not talked of at the beginning of the century.
We usually referred to a certain term used in the French
Revolution. As a result of higher standards in education and the
economic media, there's been a change in the centre of gravity of
power, public opinion. The ordinary people are much better
informed now than they were, and less inclined to accept
willy-nilly the view of their government. I think the Vietnam war
was the first example of a full-blown war that was ended by
public opinion, in mid-stream. The regime in Spain was altered
by public opinion, also the Portuguese regime. We've had the fall
of the colonels in Greece and in Cuba the power of the people has
changed governments. A less pleasant example to think about,
but nevertheless true, is what happened in Iran.
      Public opinion does influence the government in the Soviet
Union and that's quite interesting, it tends to come mainly
through the satellite countries like Poland or East Germany on
the question of nuclear weapons. There's a very strong anti-
nuclear movement in Germany, backed up by the Churches and
young people. The demonstrations haven't spread to the Soviet
Union but the feeling has. I think the penny has dropped with
the Soviets since Afghanistan, which was a disastrous failure;
there's been a demand for material on what's going on from the
Russian people, and of course the foreign-language services have
a tremendous influence. In the Soviet Union they listen to the
BBC and the Voice of America, and in the West people listen to
Radio Moscow, so this is bringing a completely new dimension
to their own formation of opinion.

JP   If there is a race between the development of public opinion and
the build-up of nuclear arms, which will win?

SM   As soon as public opinion realizes what lunacy is going on,
matters will have to change. I mean the lunacy of the United
States and the Soviet Union controlling 50,000 nuclear warheads,
each about twenty-five times more powerful than the Hiroshima
bomb; an arsenal that could never, never, never be used. The

governments will continue for a while, in the same way as the Americans went ahead with the Vietnam war for several years, but finally public opinion will assert itself. You're going to have quite a tussle in the next few years in Europe on nuclear weapons and I'm quite sure that public opinion will win. The current demonstrations have been organized with little or no resources, by a few people like me going around the world and asking people to protest. The next step is for people to react on a longer-term basis and more thoroughly. One very important development is the attitude of the Churches; the American bishops are very strong, the Anglicans are discussing it, even the lawyers are saying that nuclear weapons are illegal.

All this has had the effect of forcing the President of the United States to come on the air practically every day to justify his military policies and the aggressiveness of American foreign policy. He does this by attacking the Russians, describing them as evil people. But this is no longer cutting much ice, and he can't start accusing the bishops of all the different countries of the world of being communist agents or anarchists. In a very short time people will refuse to vote for taxes where nuclear weapons are involved, it's beginning to take place already. People will realize that they are being taxed not in order to improve conditions of life for them, but in order to prepare for a nuclear war.

JP Could you describe some of your experiences with Amnesty International?

SM We started to build Amnesty in 1961 and the first success I think was probably the Greek colonels. We got them expelled from the Council of Europe by reason of their repressive policies. And then after that came campaigns in Spain, Portugal and so on. Currently Amnesty is regarded as the conscience of the world's public opinion, an extremely important factor. I can remember many bizarre experiences. For example, we went to see the Iranian Prime Minister under the Shah to discuss whether torture was being carried out; he said there was, but under strict supervision by experts from the United States and Britain. In other words, it was torture but it was high quality. In fact one of the more terrifying aspects of the problem is Britain's involvement in many areas of the world.

It may be true that the use of torture and the carrying out of massacres has gone on for some time but we notice it now because our media cover the world. I'm convinced, however, that there's a good deal to be said for the argument that the progress of all violence in the world arises from our acceptance of nuclear war; once you accept the eventual possibility of destroying the human race completely you tend to become demoralized and will resort to any form of cruelty and violence. I'd also make the point that we should be more afraid of mediocrities than of villains; villains can usually be exposed.

JP You're a lawyer but you have many times operated outside the law as it then stood. When, in your opinion, is law-breaking justified?

SM It's very hard to quantify or draw a line. Taking a concrete example: if you are a black South African where conditions are such that half the children die before they reach the age of four or five, then I think you are entitled to use force to get rid of the regime that imposes those conditions of life on people. It's a question of degree, and the kind of way in which a law is being broken. People may demonstrate for too long or block the traffic – that's a minor way of breaching the law; it's very different when people take to throwing hand-grenades in the streets. It depends on the circumstances.

When I was fighting in Ireland it was a war of liberation. We were entitled to try and get rid of British rule and free ourselves, and the whole country took that viewpoint. In the 1920s period the IRA had the backing of the entire Irish people, eighty or ninety per cent; the majority is merely the expression of the degree to which injustices are being perpetrated. The test is really a question of whether the injustices are such that it is inevitable that you have to overthrow the regime. In other words, are you entitled to defend yourself? The next question is whether the violence should be used in excess of what is absolutely essential. Unless human rights can be adequately protected by a rule of law then violence will inevitably follow; quite a neat simple statement. A man has the right to overturn the regime which is imposing an unjust system on him and his group or society.

JP   How would you define an 'outsider'?

SM   Somebody who is able to influence thinking and actions by people without being actually in charge of a government or part of the establishment. I've never wanted to be part of the establishment, and possibly be freer to criticize and say what I think. I was probably a bit seduced by being a member of the government; one got a false sense of power which is very dangerous, very dangerous, I enjoyed the possibility of doing things, but there was always the danger of being intolerant of criticism; I've been very careful not to regard myself as being infallible or irreplaceable.

2 Helen Suzman

When Helen Suzman was telephoned at the South African parliament in Cape Town and asked to appear in 'The Outsiders' series she replied with a polite, 'Are you sure you've got the right person?' The response had more to do with humility than an attempt at coyness, and is a fairly reliable indication of the lady's character.

As a liberal in a conservative, white society with a fascist regime she has time and again been attacked and abused. As a woman and a Jew in a male-dominated and racist state she is most certainly an outsider – perhaps never more so than today, ironically, when so many in the majority population embrace the ideas of revolution

Her family, the Gavronskys, came to South Africa in 1904, part of a massive Jewish emigration from Eastern Europe (her people were from Lithuania) which was to settle in London, New York, Johannesburg, Buenos Aires and any city which would at least tolerate their religion. Helen Gavronsky was born in 1917, underwent a convent education and mixed in an exclusively Anglo-Jewish world where blacks were only seen as servants and Afrikaners hardly seen at all. At the age of nineteen, after studying at the University of the Witwatersrand, she met and married Moses Meyer Suzman. They have two daughters.

Always a bright student, she began to lecture during the war and became popular as an approachable, amusing and attractive teacher. At the same time privileged eyes were being opened. The South African Institute of Race Relations asked her to join their organization and in 1947 sent her as a delegate to a conference on human rights in London.

Now realizing that social change would only come about through politics she joined the United Party of Jan Smuts in the early fifties. In 1953 she was elected as member of parliament for Houghton. The party was changing, however, abandoning any sense of realistic opposition, and it soon became obvious that the liberals in and out of the assembly would have to have a separate voice and organization. The 1961 election was fought by the new Progressive Party. It was obliterated; Helen Suzman was now its sole representative.

For the next thirteen years hers was the only voice of genuine opposition to the policies of apartheid in the South African parliament. With no allies and with much open hostility she often spent up to twelve hours a day in the assembly; in an early session of 104 days she made 66 speeches, 26 amendments and asked 137 questions. During the committee stages of the General Law Amendment Bill she made over twenty speeches and moved amendments to sixteen clauses.

Her visits to both black and white political prisoners kept hopes alive, reassured those behind bars that they were not completely alone and forgotten. Her role became easier with the formation of the Progressive Federal Party and consequent election of more 'liberal' members of parliament; but with this success in a challenging political climate came criticism of Suzman and her supporters by a new, younger breed of liberal.

Anti-apartheid campaigner, writer and politician Peter Hain praises Helen Suzman's courage but questions here current policies. 'She's been a doughty supporter of human dignity and I certainly respect the woman. But I remember her opposing me on television when we were organizing the 'Stop the Seventy Tour'. Today it's universally agreed that the campaign was successful. You see I feel that the authentic liberals were crushed by the early 1960s. You have to ask if her liberalism could really stop apartheid.'

Perhaps Hain is right, but it is also true that, during her years of sole parliamentary opposition, Helen Suzman not only kept the spark of liberal thought alive inside the South African system, she also demonstrated to the Western world that not every white in the country was a racist, and helped to prevent the complete alienation of the black population – no mean achievement. It could perhaps be argued that Helen Suzman loves the victims of oppression more than she hates those who oppress; whether this is a bad thing is open to question. What is not open to question is her profound sense of decency.

JP   You were the effective opposition in the assembly for thirteen years, but there must have been times when you felt that you were deceiving yourself – sitting in a cosy chamber debating racism.

HS   I was trying to allow nothing to go by default. I wasn't prepared to allow any of these laws which permitted detention without trial, for instance, to go through parliament without an opposing voice because the then official opposition, to its eternal shame, gave the green light to the government on many of these contentious issues. The other thing was of course to try to put a brake on the tightening up of the apartheid laws, whether they applied to coloured people, to Indian people or black people, and there were many of those during the sixties and early seventies, which were the years when I was alone.

One tried to draw the distinction between a real democracy and a country in which seventy-two per cent of the people are denied the vote; eighty per cent, in fact, if you include coloured and Indian people. So you know, one made no attempt to tell the government in any way that the system was satisfactory from a democratic point of view, quite the opposite. One was using parliament to try and reveal all the time the terrible shortcomings of the system, and I would say that you don't have much alternative when you live there if you're a liberally minded South African, to use it in its best sense. A lot of people have left, but if you stay out there and you want to fight the system, well then you've got to use whatever methods are available to you; and if you're not part of a revolutionary movement, parliament is the major forum, and the opposition part in parliament is the major political weapon that you have to use.

JP But for this you were the receiver of a great deal of blind hatred and abuse. It must have taken courage to continue when you were alone.

HS There were of course unpleasant remarks and some of them were anti-semitic. I remember when I first went into parliament there was an old nationalist front-bencher who used to say 'Go back to Moscow' every time I stood up to speak. And then it was changed later to 'Go back to Israel' when there was a bit of anti-semitism floating around. But then, after the Six Day War, Israel was too good for me – so I was sent back to Moscow again, you see, and funnily enough I actually got there in 1982. I sent the Minister of Law and Order a card. I addressed it to 'Dear Comrade LeFranche, plenty of law and order here,' but he claims he never received the card, so it is either with the KGB or the security police in South Africa, I'm not sure which.

As to being brave, I don't know. I would say that courage is doing something when you're terribly frightened and I can't ever say that I was terribly frightened of parliament, because I was after all a duly elected member and I had a right to talk and the right to enter debates and so on. There were times when it was a bit scary, when Dr Verwoerd was around, because he was really a pretty frightening man. You know he had a sort of divine mission and that always makes people very difficult to deal with.

JP We hear a great deal about the so-called homelands. What happens to those people who are dumped there?

HS Of course the Minister of Co-operation and Development would immediately object to the use of the word 'dumped' and would say that that no longer takes place. It's about the control of people really and it's essentially a discriminatory law because it doesn't apply to coloured people, people of mixed birth and it doesn't apply to South African Asians, except that they're not allowed to enter the Orange Free State. These days the Minister will tell you that they do not move people until they have supplied certain essentials such as water, lots of latrines and a school and sometimes a clinic, and that's it. And when the people get there they have to rebuild their houses. They're sometimes given tents in which they live for a certain amount of months while they're trying to build their houses, but you must remember that in the main these are women and children and old men who are being moved, the younger men are generally migrant workers in the cities.

Now I wouldn't know how to start to build my own house I must tell you. Even if you gave me all the materials and the specifications I would find it very difficult and I'm sure that they do too. The government provides rations for three days so I asked last year what happens on the fourth day; because these people are now in an area which is strange to them and they haven't established themselves there. Maybe they have lost the jobs they had in the old nearby cities or towns, and they're there, many of them, living on pensions. It's one of the cruellest aspects, I believe, of the whole apartheid system and about two million people have already been moved under this. Until the removal system is abolished completely it's very difficult to talk about real reform in South Africa.

JP You're one of the few people who have been able to visit Nelson Mandela and you've also kept up contact with his wife Winnie.

HS Yes, well the last time I visited him was about a year ago and he was in very good health and very good spirits. He's quite a remarkable person, I mean there's nothing cringing about this man although he's been in gaol for twenty years. He is a very forthright person and clearly very much in control of the situation. He's had my support as a prisoner although I don't necessarily agree with his or Winnie's views but that's by the way, it's unimportant to me. The important thing is he is there, he's got a life sentence and one of my jobs I believe is to keep an eye on prisoners. And particularly those people who've been sentenced for what the government prefers to call crimes against the state but who are known as political prisoners by other people.

JP Some people will say that as long as there's a profit to be made in South Africa the system of apartheid will survive. It's also the case that the British government has stopped publishing a blacklist of British companies that pay African workers starvation wages.

HS I do think they ought to continue to publicize the names of firms that are paying wages that are too low. There are of course a number of firms now which say they apply the Sullivan Principles, which mean better conditions of work, use of blacks in managerial positions and so on, and negotiation with black trade unions. But the old capitalism-and-apartheid-go-hand-in-hand argument isn't true, although there was a lot in it many years ago when South Africa relied almost entirely on the primary industries of mining and agriculture, and people wanted cheap unskilled labour which they got in considerable supply from the homelands or native reserves as they were then called. I don't think that applies today to nearly the same extent, in fact it's industrialists that want the change, they want to be able to use skilled, black labour and the major opposition to that has come not from the capitalists but from the white trade unions.

JP   What are your feelings about sanctions? It sounds as though you don't approve of them.

HS   Well, first of all I don't think they're realistic, you're not going to have a full-scale economic boycott of South Africa. It's just not on: number one, it's too difficult to apply, and number two, it might well be counter-productive. And I'm not going into the argument that blacks lose their jobs first. They do, but then most blacks will say to you, we don't care, bring on sanctions and it will hasten the whole change in the South African system. The pillars of the system are, as far as I'm concerned, things like the Group Areas Act, which is a residential segregation act, and the race-classification act, which puts people into categories of race at birth and there they remain for the rest of time unless they get themselves transferred (and they are very few). And then there is the pass-law system which prevents mobility of black people, and the homeland system which I've already spoken about. These are the pillars, not the use of black workers in industry. I mean that's the only thing that's raising standards of living for them. Once you've gone you lose all influence, and there's going to be a vacuum which somebody will fill who probably cares even less. You'll get other countries stepping in who may have lower standards. If it's punitive that's a different thing. A lot of people want the boycotts, especially the sports boycott, for nothing other than a punitive reason.

JP   How does the white liberal such as yourself in South Africa deal with the charge of hypocrisy, that embodied in white liberalism is the very privilege that shores up the system of apartheid?

HS   I don't know that one tries to answer that question. It's generally an accusation rather, that is put by radical people who believe that liberals in South Africa are a bulwark against revolution, and the sooner everything collapses the better, because then there will be a whole new regime in South Africa. I don't go along with that and I don't reply to charges of hypocrisy because I don't think that I'm a hypocrite. I do what I can do. It's limited. I'm the first one to admit it, and, secondly, I know I'm a privileged white who can afford to wait longer for change than the black man who is suffering all the indignities and hardships of apartheid. But you can only do what you can do within the system, and I am there actually in South Africa, while the charges come largely from people living many thousands of miles away who think that the revolution will come, and come soon, and be completely successful. I don't believe that is going to be the case.

They say that my very presence and those like me bolsters up the system of apartheid, just the very fact that we're there and not working against the system in a really radical way. Well I believe change is going to come about via the economics of the situation; in other words, as blacks take over the skilled work in South Africa or become the majority of the skilled workers as I'm sure they will do in due course. One must realize that in the country there is a very sophisticated army, there is a para-military force, there is the police force and there are very many informers among the black people themselves. Together with the oppressive system of detention without trial all this makes it very difficult to get any really aggressive movement going in South Africa. You realize that political organizations like the African National Congress and the Pan African Congress are banned organizations, and that a great number of the leaders are banned themselves or in exile. There is urban violence and I believe that is going to increase. Something like 4,000 young people are estimated to have left South Africa after the Soweto unrest and have gone into other countries for training. And certainly some of them have come back again and have been responsible for acts of violence. But it takes much more than that to put a regime out of power.

JP   But why should a black South African living as he does agree with you? Why shouldn't he say that he has nothing to lose and that bloodshed is the only answer?

HS   Well I think he does have something to lose. He has his life and maybe that's the deterrent. Or maybe he realizes he can be locked up for a long time without recourse to the courts of law. I don't like violence of any kind, I don't like it whether it comes from people who are fighting the regime and I also don't like it when it's institutionalized violence that comes from the government. But the Soweto riots proved very conclusively that you cannot fight armoured cars with stones. It isn't a case of accepting it, it's what is possible, and in a country like South Africa armed rebellion would result in tremendous, terrible bloodshed and the whole thing is not going to happen that way.

JP   What do you think black South Africans want today, and how do they regard Helen Suzman?

HS   I can't speak for the majority of blacks – I don't know whether I can speak for any blacks – but I would imagine that there is still a large section of the black population that realizes that South Africa needs whites just as South Africa needs blacks in order to maintain the standards and improve them. And certainly the black people that I've talked to don't talk about pushing the whites into the sea. They talk about co-operation with whites. There are, however, radicals who probably think quite different- ly, and they want nothing except a black majority government and that's it.
        I sometimes think I'm an anachronism and I know some of the younger people think that and don't rate me highly at all. The older ones still have a very considerable understanding of what I'm trying to do, and I get well received when I go to Soweto and visit those people.

JP   What is the future? What do you think South Africa will be like in ten years time, as opposed to what you hope it will be like in ten years time?

HS   I think it's going to change much more gradually than I would like to see it change. But I still believe that it will roll on with better living conditions for blacks, in the urban areas anyway. Perhaps greater realization that you can't just shove people around without the world reacting to it, and therefore I hope that there will be something freezing removals. The blacks will learn how to use what power they do have, both economic power and the power they are going to be given in local government, and I believe the country will just go on developing in that way with changes coming in the socio-economic field rather more rapidly than anything in the political field for black people. Some whites are becoming more frightened and a lot of young people have left, which is perhaps a very distressing part of it all.

I'd like a change in the system so that black South Africans do not have to get up at 4.30 in the morning to travel from Soweto which is about fifteen miles out of Johannesburg to go to work in very over-crowded trains and earn low wages and be stopped by the police at any time and asked to produce a document showing that they have a right to be in the city. And I want to end the bullying really, the bullying that goes on in that country – in my country I should say. I hate to see defenceless people being knocked around. I really hate it, and this is what happens and it's very upsetting indeed.

3 Martha Gelhorn

Martha Gellhorn is an American exile dividing her time between travelling, which is her abiding love, a flat in London and a cottage in Wales. She is an elegant woman, seemingly as at home behind a cigarette holder as she is behind a typewriter reporting a war in Vietnam, telling of the horrors of a Nazi death camp or composing a novel. She has travelled to fifty-three countries, lived in seven of them, and since 1936 has contributed some of the most vivid and challenging journalism to come out of any war.

Born in St Louis, her father was a doctor and mother a campaigner for female suffrage. She always had an urge to travel and, while on a trip with her mother, met Ernest Hemingway whom she was later to marry. He dedicated *For Whom the Bell Tolls* to her and they worked in Spain together, but the marriage did not last.

She learned her craft during the Spanish Civil War, feeling, along with many of her contemporaries, that here was the place to stop fascism, the battleground of democracy. The anecdotes from the period are, of course, legion; it is said, though unconfirmed, that the first time friends realized that Martha and Hemingway were lovers was when a shell hit their hotel and both correspondents ran from the same room. She worked extensively for *Collier's* at the time, filing impressive copy and earning a reputation as a pertinent and discerning writer.

It was also in the 1930s that she worked for Harry Hopkins and the Federal Emergency Relief Administration, surveying how people were existing in the depression. She collected these reports in *The Trouble I've Seen*, and troubles they certainly were. With film-star looks, high intelligence and a disrespect for authority she caused quite a stir as she encountered poverty and suffering, and tried to explain the situation to the Federal Government.

In 1938 she wrote from Czechoslovakia of the democratic nature of the country and warned of the Nazi threat. After covering the Finnish war she travelled to various fronts during the Second World War, finally entering

Dachau concentration camp with the liberating troops. After 1945 she reported from the Middle Eastern campaigns and then went to Vietnam where she produced much of her best work.

Phillip Knightley, author of the definitive book on war reporting, *The First Casualty*, says of her, 'After the Spanish war, where she was still learning and suffered from being with Hemingway, she became one of the best, no doubt. It wasn't easy being a woman because the generals of the time were reluctant to have females anywhere near the front line. Montgomery wouldn't allow women correspondents even after the Normandy landings. In Vietnam she achieved remarkable things. I mean, what do you do if you're an American covering a war with about 500 other people and it's not a war you approve of? She decided to investigate the United States' claim that they were trying to win the hearts and minds of the Vietnamese people; she went out to discover how the civilian population were reacting. The articles were so good and so accusing that she often had a lot of difficulty finding someone brave enough to publish them.'

She has written many books, including *The Honeyed Peace*, *Travels with Myself and Another*. In spite of a wisdom which she expresses eloquently, her modesty is such that she sometimes shows a lack of confidence in her own ability – a refreshing but erroneous stance. She is a valued friend and a fine journalist.

JP You wrote the book *The Trouble I've Seen* in 1936 at the time of the New Deal. Could you describe the depression and your experiences at the time?

MG What I was doing was working for Harry Hopkins who was then head of the Federal Emergency Relief Administration, and I trundled around the country reporting to him on how relief was working. Relief was a type of dole; there hadn't been anything like it up to that time; you just starved. I talked to people, saw how they were treated and submitted reports. You see, when the depression happened people had no means of livelihood, they just sold apples or begged or died. Under the new scheme you were asked all sorts of questions, very searching questions often asked in a nasty way. They got it by the week, and hated taking charity because that was a terrible thing to have to do in America. Their pride was destroyed, they were no longer independent people.

A lot of people moved towards the cities to try to get jobs, and they lived in shanties made out of corrugated tin and called Hoovervilles. This was something brand-new and horrible. In the South they were living on subsistence farms; it astonished me how they could have lived before the depression but now they'd really had it. They didn't have enough money to buy grain or plant anything, they'd sold their mule or eaten it as the case may be, and their houses were in conditions of absolutely black misery with four to a room. People were so shaken and hurt that they were peaceful. Nobody revolted or rioted or did anything because they took it as if it was their fault. It was pitiful, awful.

I think the shame of the situation was probably an American attitude, because it's a country where everybody is very proud of always standing on their own feet and making good. Actually it was the only real hardship America had known since the civil war and it's the only thing anybody remembers; you know, they've never been bombed, never been invaded and they've forgotten the civil war except in the South where they're all loopy. I was angry, angry for them, and I suppose I was shocked as well at the humiliation of it all.

The difference between then and now is that we had Roosevelt and his wife, and she was a great influence on him and his policy. It was recognized that what was going on was wrong and bad, there was no feeling that it was OK to have so-and-so many unemployed. When he said there was nothing to fear but fear itself, it meant a great deal. This wasn't a natural disaster; there was no enemy; the system had just packed in for those mysterious reasons of economics. I don't believe the New Deal was at all cynical, brought in to prevent an uprising. Americans are very slow to rise up and I think the government in the mid-thirties was a good government. In Britain today it's a different story. Nobody who's actually administering aid will talk to you because of official secrets and people are paid enough to keep them from starving and from rioting presumably.

There's one fairly ridiculous story from that time. I was in a little town called Curdalene, Idaho. The unemployed were given a job to shovel mud from one place to another but the contractor who supplied the shovels collected them and threw them away some place so the next day they had no work. They were very distressed about this and I told them the only way to get any attention is to break the windows of the relief office, somebody will come and pay attention. We got some beer, talked about it, and then they went off and did it. Their beef was taken care of but I was recalled to Washington by the FBI and fired for inciting revolution. It didn't worry me because I wanted to write a book instead of continuing with the job, and as I was clearing out my office the telephone rang and it was the President's secretary saying that the President and Mrs Roosevelt were very worried about me and thought it'd be a good idea if I lived in the White House until I found some sort of work. I did.

JP You've reported on many wars, and in your book *The Face of War* you said that people are either sheep or tigers, we are all guilty of stupidity and therefore we must expect wars and shall never be free of them. What did you mean by that?

MG I hate stupidity as original sin and we've all got it and those who lead us have probably got it worst. I'm talking about stupidity of thinking as well as stupidity of feeling. The leaders trot out their stupidities and we follow or we don't follow; those who follow the cruel stupidities are the tigers and those who allow themselves to be led to the slaughter are the sheep. We get stupidity from the top by osmosis. I used to think that people were responsible for their leaders, but not any more. I'm not saying we're lemmings, I'm saying we're victims. It's hard enough just living your life and using thought and energy; to take up a position takes a lot of time.

But individuality and the courage and bravery of people is amazing isn't it, it almost makes me take everything back. In El Salvador just now some kids are running a thing called the commission of human rights. They're kids, I mean in their twenties, and they work in a shack behind an office collecting information on murders, torture, kidnappings and disappearances connected with the government security forces. It's the most dangerous work possible, any one of them on the way home could be picked up and found dead in a garbage dump alongside the road. Nobody rewards them, and the moral and physical guts to do this are colossal. So it's unjust I suppose to suggest that we're just victims and victimizers, it's governments I take off against. Tolstoy said governments are a collection of men who do violence to the rest of us, and that's about right. They're all bad, and some are worse.

JP In Spain you and many other people grew up politically; why was that?

MG We were on the side of the Republic, which had been a legally elected government which was attacked by the military, aided and abetted by Mussolini and Hitler. We observed the attitudes of the democracies who abandoned Spain; in fact the British government was the greatest criminal in that it invented non-intervention, and that didn't harm Franco and company but it totally starved the Republic. So we started to see how the world worked, observed the crookedness and the stupidity. And yes, we were naive in the sense that we didn't expect these things to happen. But we were all anti-fascist and had seen it in Germany and Italy, and knew what fascism was and that it had to be stopped.

It was a lot easier then, a lot more clear. There was a definite enemy and we knew that if he wasn't stopped in Spain it'd have to be done later on in Europe. For that we were called fellow travellers or cassandras or whatever, but lo and behold it came about. You see it was a unique war in that so many reporters were there and we all witnessed the bravery, the incredible bravery of the people. The only thing that finished them was hunger, the hospitals were full of starving children and people would queue for ages for just one orange. We were objective, you must understand that, but we were also involved with the fate of the Republic. I was there a very long time and every day there was something that moved and impressed me.

JP You've observed 'reds under the bed' policies in the Spanish war, under McCarthy and today against the anti-nuclear movement. Can you compare them?

MG It's not as ludicrous now as it used to be. Senator McCarthy did permanent and lasting damage in America with all the loyalty oaths and that kind of thing. It's a neurosis I think; if you reach the point where you can suggest that the CND or the same movements in America are slaves of the Kremlin, or paid by them or something, you really have to be neurotic or a nut-case. There is a deep-seated fear of Russian communism, as if it was so attractive and so powerful that given an inch it would sweep the world, when in fact it's profoundly unattractive and anybody who's been treated to a taste of it only wants out. And the idea that they're so immensely clever and subtle and brilliant that all the rest of us have to be shivering for fear of them I find a joke. But Mr Reagan does it every minute of the week. I remember him saying that unless we saved El Salvador for a monstrous government and a monstrous ruling class, the Kremlin would be sitting on the Panama Canal. I'd roar with laughter if it wasn't that people believed this rubbish.

Americanism is something I don't quite understand, with the moral majority and people wearing American flags in their lapels. It seems to be some sort of mindless answer to the mindless threat of communism. When I grew up in America nobody waved or ran around announcing that they were American and the best. We were quite easy-going with it and happy and calm and sure of ourselves. It's a form of excessive nationalism which must be a sign of doubt and weakness. I'm an American and I care about my country. I was against the war in Vietnam in 1966 and I'm against our intrusion into El Salvador not only on moral grounds but also because it's wrong for America and destructive of everything the country should stand for.

JP You described the conflict between China and Japan as 'the war no one knew or cared about'.

MG That's perfectly true, but as far as I was concerned the real reason I wanted to go was I thought the world was very likely going to end and I wanted to see the East before it did. Obviously one was against the Japanese and in favour of the Chinese, but my real interest was to see what Chinese people were like, what China was like. In fact it was a sort of non-war because the Japanese discovered that you could make a move of a 120 miles any time you wanted but the peasants burnt everything and retreated; there were no roads so you just had to go back. The Japanese came over and bombed all the time, there was no defence against that. I want to tell you that it is my firm opinion that anybody who invades that country is such a nut-case that they really need psychiatric care. It's enormous, enormous. And the people are perfectly capable of dying starving. It's like Russia; nobody should ever invade Russia or China and that's my contribution to military history.

JP After covering the Second World War you arrived at Dachau. Could you describe what you saw?

MG There was a train on a siding. It was a death train the SS had left, so they hadn't emptied it. Germans with handkerchiefs over their faces, under the arms of Americans who had gotten there the day before, were opening the doors of it and digging out the bodies of the people who had died in this train. That was the first thing. Then you went into the gates of the camp and you were sprayed, you opened your clothes and you were sprayed with powder against typhus lice inside. You went in and there were figures still alive in striped pyjamas, skeletons still breathing and lying and sitting about. By the furnaces there were stacked bodies, yellow, melting, the little fat still on the skeletons because they hadn't had time to burn them. In the prison cells, the torture cells there was a woman screaming; she was mad, she was alive, she was screaming. There was a bunch of women in cotton dresses, Jews, who had been sent there from some place else, who clutched one's clothes and screamed. There was the infirmary which was manned by Polish doctors who had been sort of laboratory assistants to the Germans, they were very quiet. It was a circle of hell, and you really had to say to yourself, I wonder if the human species is a bearable species.

The Poles showed me their records, they were beautifully kept and listed how long it took for a man to die when he was immersed in ice water, the results of castration, how long it takes for death after injections under the knee of certain chemicals. It was a horror, a nightmare for years to come. A very tall skeleton wearing a blanket came into the record room, he'd been dug out of that train I was speaking about. He spoke to these doctors in Polish, told them the war was over. One of them replied 'Bravo'; I said that he must have more to say than bravo, and he said, 'It's a bit late.' At that I ran out of Dachau in a state bordering on uncontrolled hysteria and went and sat in a field waiting to be removed.

I've never forgiven the Germans. Never, never. And indeed I went back to both Germany and Poland in something like 1962 or around that time, I'm very bad on dates, and spoke to students and young people who had lived free of the war. The Germans were dreadful. They may be better now, but then they couldn't understand why people were rude to them in foreign countries, tried to justify themselves as guiltless. In Poland there was a complete contrast. There was no anti-semitism left, they spoke about everything and thought freely, did extraordinary and funny things. There was no disease of respect for authority, they were perfectly wonderful.

JP At Nuremberg the Nazis were punished, but wars usually end with buck-passing. You covered Vietnam, and the United States has consistently shirked responsibility both during and after that war.

MG Yes, that's right. Some form of trial would have been the most useful thing for future military and political attitudes on the part of the United States, instead of which it's simply pushed under the rug and the unfortunate GIs who are the victims in America can go and peddle their peanuts. And the Vietnamese, who were promised apparently by Nixon something over three billion dollars in reparations, never got a penny and are instead treated to a policy of oppressive harassment. Imagine being on the side of the Khmer Rouge in the United Nations, just because of the fury of having been defeated by oriental peasants. There should have been documentation of what happened in Vietnam, but we lost the war as opposed to what happened in 1945, so there was no Nuremberg. Vietnam was based on lies, based on the domino theory which was ludicrous; after all, we aid and abet China to attack Vietnam but we fought in Vietnam to keep China out. Criminal stupidity.

JP Is war ever fun?

MG Well it can be funny. You operate on a basis of functional schizophrenia in war – you can't stand it for anybody else but yourself, yes. I found it enjoyable in the sense that I always thought I was with the best people, I loved the people I was with. I liked having no possessions, no problems, and you never knew if you were going to be alive the next day and that was immensely interesting. You couldn't really do anything but weep or laugh, normally we laughed. Wars can be black farce, for example during the Battle of the Bulge when the Germans were dressed up in American uniform and the American jeeps. Nobody knew what was happening, a small group of perfectly honest Americans were on a roof being attacked by two American planes; they were shooting back at them, and the torrent of abuse was so great that I just cowered in a corner laughing my head off.

It can also be very exhilarating, because danger starts all the adrenalin running around and if you know you've had a bit of danger and nothing happened you feel great. That's purely chemical. And of course as a reporter one is in the happy position of never having to just sit around in the mud and wait, because as soon as any action stopped you moved on. The troops meantime just had to sit, bored to death, waiting until they were called. Although my own private notes are full of soul-destroying boredom, I had comrades who were all jokers and I was madly devoted to the troops. You hated war for what it did to people, but loved being with such good people.

JP Where and who are the young Martha Gellhorns?

MG Oh there are plenty of them, of both sexes. There's never a lack of talent and there's always somebody else. There must be and thank God there are. The young who are in Friends of the Earth, the young who are fighting to keep unnecessary nuclear power stations out, and they're also there in journalism. I think the world is just as awful as it can be at any given moment, but a certain number of people appear and try to keep it from being unbearably awful. The history behind us is perfectly terrible and the history ahead will be perfectly terrible, but a few will fight like hell to keep it from being worse. The only thing that could stop this would be nuclear weapons and idiots in charge. If that doesn't happen I have some hope.

4 Wilfred Burchett

On 27 September 1983 Wilfred Burchett died in Sofia at the age of seventy-two, only a few months after being interviewed for this book. As a war correspondent of the first order his qualities were recognized all over the world, but, for Burchett, reporting the situation was not enough; if he saw an act of injustice he would do his best to remedy it. For this much loved, and at times much hated man the roads of good and evil, right and wrong were discernible – he never had any doubt about which one to take.

He grew up in Poowong in the Australian state of Victoria with a family background of hardship and loss. The depression of the 1890s had ruined his grandfather, a pioneer farmer, just as the depression in the 1930s ruined his father, at a critical time in Wilfred's life. 'The day came' wrote Wilfred in his autobiography *At the Barricades*, 'when the bank manager and his agent came to seize the house. After a few polite words to my father they began looking over the furnishings. "You can stay for a few days until you find another place," said the manager as he left. My father's face was ashen as he stumbled inside after seeing him to the gate.'

Wilfred spent the rest of his youth 'on the road' looking for work where there was none. He was adopted by a gang of cane-cutters whose spirit of one-for-all-and-all-for-one left a lasting impression on him; and if any tag applies at all, he became a tribune of an especially Australian form of radicalism which an American colleague acknowledged many years later when he said of him, 'Burchett? He's not a communist! He's an Australian.'

He travelled to Europe shortly before the outbreak of the war in 1939 and took part in a mission rescuing Jews from Nazi Germany. On his return to Australia he began his journalism by writing letter upon letter to newspapers warning of the spread of fascism. He next travelled to China, then under siege by the Japanese, and was appointed correspondent of the London *Daily Express*; and in 1945 he wrote what has been described as the 'scoop of the century'.

He was the first Western reporter to enter Hiroshima after the atomic bombing in August 1945, and his *Daily Express* front page carried the first 'warning to the world'. Above all, Wilfred Burchett was a brave man. The Brisbane *Courier-Mail* reported on 11 September 1945: 'A pocket-handkerchief-sized Australian, Wilfred Burchett, left all other correspondents standing in covering the occupation of Japan. Armed with a typewriter, seven packets of K rations, a Colt revolver and incredible hope, he made a one-man penetration of Japan and was the first correspondent into Hiroshima. (He then) embarked on his one-man liberation tour of prison camps ... even before official rescue parties reached them.'

A campaign was launched to refute Burchett's claim that radiation poisoning was a reality in Hiroshima. This was a turning point; he went on to report consistently from what was considered the 'other side', or the 'wrong side'. After spells in Hungary and China he went to Korea to cover the war, and involved himself in a controversy which is still hotly debated. He visited Australian prisoners-of-war in a North Korean camp and was falsely accused of taking part in interrogation sessions. Although he took legal action on the issue and proved his innocence, the Australian government refused to renew his passport. For many years he was forced to travel on a variety of documents, including a Cuban passport, a North Vietnamese permit and a 'laissez-passer', an enormous document which filled an attaché case.

Asia captivated him, and his first visit to Vietnam started a life-long affection for that nation and its people, which was reciprocated. He was a close friend of Ho Chi Minh, and he frequently published interviews with such men as North Vietnam's foreign minister, Nguyen Duy Trinh, and the chief of the Vietcong, Nguyen Hu Tho. It was always a feature of Burchett that all sides attacked him: he was called a KGB agent and a British spy; communist death squads planned to kill him and in Kampuchea almost did.

It is true that he did possess a naiveté which, on occasion, gave his enemies opportunities and ammunition. He was never a member of any communist organization, although he would never have denied support for various revolutionary groups. He remained the warmest and most generous of men. He wrote more than forty books and never made more than a living wage, sometimes a great deal less. After his death those with grudges rose to attack the man; and it is deeply significant that many of them did not dare to do so when their target was alive and able to deploy his courage in hitting back.

JP   When you first entered Hiroshima what did you see, what did you feel?

WB   The thing was getting to Hiroshima; that was the most difficult part because the correspondents who were recruited to MacArthur's command believed that no trains ran in Japan. It was a rather eerie sort of ride because the train was full of Japanese troops and officers. On the outside of the carriage the troops were quite all right but once in the carriage itself the officers were hostile. Each one had a terrific sword between his legs and most of them had a Samurai dagger. It was a scary feeling. I got to Hiroshima about two in the morning and even at daylight a few hours later it was misty. I walked from the station over a mile to the centre of the city; it wasn't like a bombed city, but it was as if a steam roller had just flattened everything out of existence. Then I went up to a third floor and could see about a mile or a mile and a half in each direction. There was nothing except a few factory chimneys which had been under the epicentre – they were burned but not destroyed.

    People didn't react to me, didn't react at all. It seems that they were still dazed by what had gone on. It was extraordinary, there I was wandering around with an umbrella and some sort of marine camouflaged blouse and no person stopped or spoke or exchanged the time of day. They walked around with white masks over their nose and mouth, silent. A feeling grew into me as I walked around that this is what happened in the last minute of World War Two but it would be the fate of cities all over the world in the first hours of World War Three. Of course one had no conception of bombs a thousand times as powerful as that one which killed something like 300,000 altogether; 100,000 they reckon at the time of the blast, and the rest died from radiation.

    I filed back a story for the *Daily Express* front page headed 'I write this as a warning to the world' and by a miracle it got through via a Japanese correspondent who used a Morse set to Tokyo, and then on to Yokohama where there was a transmission for the press, and there they tried to stop it. But a colleague on the *Express*, a very tough journalist, fought it out on the spot and stood over them as they actually transmitted the thing. I described radiation and what it did, and this was something which was denied.

A special press conference was called to attack my story about atomic radiation. The man in charge was the number two to the General who controlled the Manhattan project. He denied that there could be any trace of residual radiation, as he called it, and that the only reasons for the deaths were blast and burn and perhaps some radiation which escaped at the moment of the explosion of the bomb. He denied that there was anything in the soil or in metallic objects or that it was possible for people who were not even in Hiroshima to be contaminated – and I'd seen them in hospital, dying. That denial has gone on for decades, it's almost still going on. At the time I was actually accused of having fallen victim to Japanese propaganda because I visited the victims. Hiroshima changed my life in two senses: it confirmed that there is no equivalent or substitute for being on the spot as a journalist, reporting at first hand. And I became very conscious of what would happen in the event of a new world war, I became active on the question of nuclear disarmament.

JP Because of that scoop you were something of a hero to your readers in Britain and the West. But then you went behind what was called the Iron Curtain to report from the communist world. Why was that?

WB One has to go back a little in time to when President Truman announced this 'roll-back' policy, meaning that when socialists or communists came into a regime that had to be rolled back. I saw the beginning of this process in Germany and thought it was very dangerous. Well I thought it would be a good idea to look and see if these countries wanted to be rolled back, or did they want to go ahead and build new formed societies. That was Hungary, Bulgaria, Yugoslavia, Albania, a whole lot of them. And while I was there the Korean war started. Now I use the word started because you can argue for probably centuries who really started it. I went to see what was happening on the northern side of the 38th Parallel, to see if peace negotiations were really going on or whether it was a sham. The United States was talking about atom-bombing China at the time, so I felt it my duty as far as I had a newspaper public to go there and report what the dangers were.

I didn't know much about that war at all, but I was suspicious that there were interests in the United States who wanted to get a show-down. The Russians had exploded an atomic bomb in September '49, Mao had taken over in China in October of '49, I thought the war wasn't as it seemed to be. I had no particular sympathy for the North, I didn't know who had attacked whom, but there was that fear of atomic war. Because I had gone to China I was accredited to the Chinese as a correspondent and went with their delegation to cover the cease-fire. It was a very interesting situation because the American reporters knew after the first few weeks that they were being lied to by the official American briefing officers, they were faking maps and all sorts of abominable things. Journalists from the *New York Times* and *Time* magazine were asked why the fraternized with me, a correspondent on the other side. Their reply was that it was the only way to get the news of what was really going on.

JP You've said in the past that the role of journalist encompasses that of 'icebreaker' and 'bridge-builder'. That could be interpreted as meaning a go-between.

WB Yes, I think I wrote that actually in one of my less guarded moments. But it's true. The main thing is that a journalist doesn't belong to some rarefied atmosphere in which he shouldn't have opinions, and nobody is objective thank goodness because we're not machines. We have minds, we have eyes, we have ears, we have emotions. And there's a tendency to think that a journalist is a person who should never be associated with what he's covering, which is nonsense when you get to the question of war and peace. When I grew up in Australia, in the terrible days of the depression, it seemed that the government had no answer whatsoever for all the problems. There were two forces, one was communist and the other fascist and some people chose one and some the other. You can't insulate yourself when an issue might change the world. On one occasion Kissinger invited me to come and have breakfast with him and discuss Vietnam and the peace talks. He'd broken off secret talks with the North Vietnamese and he wanted to know how they were feeling and if they wanted to negotiate again. I could only give my opinion that they wanted to get a negotiated end to the war. It's an example of stepping outside of my journalistic role. I didn't go there to write a story.

Being discreet is obviously important but pretty much depends on what sort of field you're operating in, what sort of journalistic domain. If someone knew the date of the landing to open a second front during World War Two and they disclosed it then they ought to be shot, because that would be risking the lives of tens of thousands of people. A lot of the journalists accredited to the allied side at the time had that date but nobody dared jeopardize the whole operation. It's an extreme example but shows that while the job of the journalist is to get facts back to the public, exclusively if possible, there are limits.

When the question of exchange of POWs in Korea came up one of the branches of the American public-relations organization released a report that there was no point in having any talks because the North Koreans had massacred all the American prisoners. There were cries to drop atom bombs on Peking and all over the place. The head of the Associated Press from Tokyo came to see me and said he didn't believe the story. One of their photographers, Pappy Noel, was on a POW list. Why not send him a camera to prove either way what had happened? I asked the Chinese, they said OK, if Associated Press didn't mind risking a camera and film. So within ten days the press was carrying pictures of prisoners of war playing baseball and basketball. The talks got started, lists of prisoners were exchanged and the first man on the list was a General Dean, a divisional commander. The Americans said this proved that the whole thing was a swindle, they had absolute evidence that Dean was dead. The United Press, who were suffering badly at the hands of the AP, asked if I'd go and get photographs of General Dean and prove he was still alive. I got ambushed and shot at but I brought back pictures of Dean playing chess with the guards. And this became a double-page spread in the *Stars and Stripes*, General Dean eating with chop sticks and exercising, the whole works. The editor of *Stars and Stripes* was sacked, and General Ridgway issued an order that there must be no more fraternization. But a delegation was eventually sent from the journalists and Ridgway had to withdraw the order.

JP The Korean war was also the time of the greatest trauma of your career. After accumulating a few enemies as well as admirers along the way, you were accused of taking part in the brainwashing of Australian prisoners.

WB   Well it's rather complex. The Australian authorities reported a soldier 'killed in action' and then his name turned up on a POW list broadcast by the North Koreans. The editor of the *Melbourne Sun* passed a message asking me, because I could report from the North, to find out if this chap was alive and if so to visit him. He was alive, so I wrote to him and he replied that I should visit if I was in those parts. So I went to see him. I don't know if there were five or six of them, but they were very hostile. They'd come to Korea to kill communists they said, and they'd kill me if they could. And how could white men live on rice? I told them that the villages had been napalmed and agriculture had come to a stop. Then I wrote to the man's mother, informed the *Melbourne Sun* and even got them better food. The conversation lasted about three minutes flat, and then I was accused of brainwashing.

The Australian government took away my passport for seventeen years, until December 1972 when Mr Whitlam was elected Prime Minister. An international committee was formed to support me and put pressure on the government, a petition was signed by an international elite, people like Bertrand Russell and Jean-Paul Sartre. What actually happened was that I lost my passport on the way back from a conference in Hanoi and the Australians refused to replace it. To actually physically leave Hanoi I was given what they call a 'laissez-passer', a document which identifies you. But I had to obtain a visa for every country I went to, so that in the end I had this enormous pass which I had bound and carried in a separate case. In Cuba, where I was attending a conference, I couldn't get it into the slip where passports are meant to go. This came to Castro's ears, he invited me for lunch and then offered me a Cuban passport – which I used for some time. But what really hurt during that time was that they also denied Australian citizenship to my children. That hurt.

They even threatened airlines that they would have their licence withdrawn if they carried me. A French airline was told this when I wanted to go from New Caledonia to Australia. Eventually a newspaper proprietor sent a small plane for me. This was during Vietnam, and apparently they thought, quite wrongly, that I was going to do a long Australian-wide tour speaking about involvement in the war. Two days after I got back to Melbourne a question was asked in the House about whether I was going to be prosecuted; and the Attorney-General said there were no grounds. So you see I was really vindicated. And an extreme right-wing newspaper picked up a statement from some Soviet defector who said he'd recruited me as a KGB agent; they reported that I wasn't really a journalist at all but an agent. So I sued them, won the case, but lost it as far as costs were concerned because they decided on the judge's instructions that it had been a fair report of something which had been published in a newspaper and not in itself libel. It was a ridiculous time, difficult and unpleasant for me. It was discovered that in the huge apartment block in which I lived in Moscow there also lived a film star, a woman I'd never met. In Australia the press said 'Burchett lives with . . .'

JP You've described Vietnam as your obsession. You lived with the Vietcong, knew Ho Chi Minh, and your involvement was quite unprecedented.

WB When I met Ho Chi Minh I got my concept of what the Vietnamese are, what Vietnamese people are like. As far as I'm concerned he's the greatest man I've ever met; with all the modesty and simplicity that goes with greatness and the capacity to use some image to explain a complicated situation because he disciplined himself to talk in a language that everyone knew. I liked him straight away, and found that the case he presented, the reason they were fighting, was just. They were in a war against the French then, but the same reasoning applied with the Americans: they simply wanted their own country. Before this I'd seen many forms of communism, Chinese, Yugoslav, Soviet and the three parties that had grown in Australia. But this was not my business, although I won't deny a sense of disillusionment.

I became particularly disillusioned with the Chinese after they supported the same side as the CIA in Angola, but I put that down to China being a long way from Southern Africa, they weren't clued up on this. It was incorrect. I was shocked when China invaded Vietnam, when Pol Pot's Cambodia fought Vietnam, the two countries at each other's throats. I knew that the Vietnamese had helped a great deal in the fight against the old regime of Lon Nol, but Pol Pot announced that the war was run entirely by the Khmer Community party, of which he was leader. Then I was put on one of Pol Pot's death lists and I was ambushed. He was right, knowing his morality, to try and kill me. I knew about the horror and the massacres and I was known as an expert on Cambodia. With his primitive mind the easiest thing was to try to shoot me.

JP   You grew up in Poowong in the State of Victoria. What was the feeling of your early life, and how did that mould your career?

WB   I grew up in a sort of Methodist family, my father was a local preacher and we were taught to be correct. You didn't cheat, you didn't steal, you were good to your neighbours. We were given moral and human values, they've been a great help and I don't think I've ever parted from them. I served an apprenticeship as a carpenter but there was no work around so I tramped about like so many thousands of other young people. There was no prospect of having a job, things weren't getting better. I couldn't even dream of having what you'd call a steady girlfriend. A few of us got together and went around the country doing odd agricultural work, from bagging potatoes down in Victoria to cutting cane up in Queensland.

In Queensland I realized what could be done if there was co-operation. The cane-cutting teams were groups of men who'd share what they earned exactly; if there were ten of them and there was £100, it was £10 each. They were good people, people I could get along with and admire. There was no contradiction between their ways and what I'd been taught at Sunday School. If someone wasn't fit he would take time off and still be given wages. I remember that you could tell how much cane each man had cut by the size of the pile behind him. I remarked to one man that his pile was twice the size of the next cutter's. 'Well,' he said, 'we're mates. Not dingoes.' That made quite an impression on me.

Later I learnt a few languages from books and went to England to get a job with a tourist company. I married a German Jewish refugee girl in London, and her brother had been arrested in an early pogrom in November 38. I decided, rashly, to go over and get him out. That was one incident which perhaps fixed my style of journalism. I saw what was happening, saw what Nazism did to people and when I went back to Australia with my new wife I wrote to the papers about it. You see Robert Menzies, who was later to be Prime Minister, was Premier of Victoria and he made speeches about Hitler being a man of peace and all this. Of course the newspapers wouldn't touch my letters at that time; but after the war broke out they printed them, and asked me to write articles. I've been involved ever since.

JP   Have you ever felt a sense of regret?

WB   No, no I can't say I have. I might have done things a bit differently, but no regrets. It's been tough on my family, on my children. Not only because of the political stigma and so forth but because I've been away from home so much; they've suffered more than they would ever tell me. You've got to be able to look your children in the eye and look at yourself and not be ashamed. As to the tags and names, well I'm not a communist. Not that I dislike or despise them, but because I've never taken a party line. I'm an independent radical, anything else would be out of line with my concept of reporting. You've got to be able to get off in time and say: 'Well there it is, I was wrong.'

5 Jessica Mitford

A family photograph of the young Jessica Mitford shows a slightly podgy, long-haired child wearing a buttoned coat, a large hat and a grimace. But there's more. The full cheeks and turned-down mouth belie a determined character which, even at an early age, was reacting and questioning. The arms are folded carefully, the posture is challenging, almost angry; it is a portrait of miniature defiance.

There has been little change over the years. The lady had seen a lot, experienced much and possibly mellowed accordingly. She is still a rebel though, still fighting her good fight and searching for the bad guys. And she does it with an endearing wit and charm and a quality which is, sadly, not always typical of the contemporary Left: she has a lust, as well as a concern, for life.

The youngest daughter of Lord and Lady Redesdale was born in 1917 into a privileged family which, until the 1930s, had not been too eccentric by English upper-class standards to be considered particularly notorious. The Mitford sisters were to change all that. In her first volume of autobiography, entitled *Hons and Rebels*, Jessica tells of the lives of the family members in an environment where 'to my father, outsiders included not only Huns, Frogs, Americans, blacks and all other foreigners, but also other people's children, the majority of my older sisters' acquaintances, almost all young men – in fact, the whole teeming population of the earth's surface . . .'

It is a book thought to be a model of its kind, characterized by humour and an understanding of friends and enemies alike. The latter occupied much of Decca's (her final nickname, adopted by the entire family) life until she left home. Unity, three years older, was a close companion and constant opponent. She later became a Nazi, joined Hitler's circle in Germany and attempted suicide when Britain declared war.

Nancy was the eldest, and skips through the life of the family in flashes of laughter and more than a little brilliance. Her novels were, and are, very successful. Diana also joined the extreme right, marrying British fascist leader Sir Oswald Mosley. Deborah and Pamela did not rival their three sisters in terms of worldly fame, and did not seem to desire to do so. Deborah is now the Duchess of Devonshire, Pamela married a respected scientist and is the 'unknown' Mitford sister. Brother Tom died during the Second World War.

Decca's progressive instincts appeared early, and she recalls as a child asking her mother why all the money in England couldn't be divided up equally amongst everybody, thereby eliminating poverty. 'Well, that's what the socialists want to do', replied her mother and explained away the apparent iniquity of society. The dissuasion was only temporary. With her sisters becoming increasingly committed to the right, Decca became a radical.

In 1937 at the age of nineteen she ran away to Spain with Esmond Romilly, whom she later married and had a daughter by. Romilly was Winston Churchill's nephew and there is a tendency to dismiss him as a young romantic; it is one of the few areas where Jessica Mitford becomes rather sensitive, defending the reputation of a man who was killed while with the Canadian Air Force in 1941. By this time Jessica had settled in America, fearing and disliking the political attitudes of the British establishment.

She joined the American Communist Party in 1943, and wrote about this vital period of her life in *A Fine Old Conflict*, the second instalment of her memoirs. The title comes from a misunderstanding of the opening line of 'The Internationale' – ''Tis the final conflict.' 'For some years, before I saw the words written down,' she says in the introduction to the book, 'I thought it began: "It's a fine old conflict . . ." which to me it was then and ever shall be.' It was in Washington that she met her second husband Bob Treuhaft, a lawyer of Hungarian Jewish origin. They were to devote themselves to revolutionary politics until leaving the Communist Party in 1956.

But it is her journalism which has made the biggest impact, delighting and provoking almost everybody who reads it in magazine, newspaper or book form. Apart from a remarkable collection of articles entitled 'The Making of a Muckraker' and incisive works on the United States prison system and 'The Trial of Dr Spock', in 1963 she published *The American Way of Death*. It's one of the most important investigative books yet written, condemning with vigour and humour the funeral business and exposing exploitation and absurdity. The book provoked legal reforms on the subject, and more than one offer of a 'free funeral' for the author from less than grateful undertakers.

She lives in Oakland, California with her husband, working long hours and smoking the strongest kind of cigarette with an almost arrogant disregard for medical opinion. Her daughter by her first marriage works as a nurse, son Benjy Treuhaft is a piano tuner; she has two grandchildren by her daughter's marriage to the black radical James Forman. The cut-glass accent hasn't changed but her views are as forward-thinking as ever. Carl Bernstein, the Watergate reporter, described her as follows: 'Having a winsome manner, an unfailing ear and an instinct for the jugular, she sets on her merry way looking very much the picture of a slightly dotty English lady.'

JP Could you give a picture of what it was like growing up with the Mitford family in what was, after all, a state of extraordinary privilege?

JM Well of course it didn't seem like that, we were always kept very short of money. It's odd, both at Swinbrook and Asthall, which were the country houses of my father, we had vast estates with ten servants in the house not including nanny and the governess, but we were always considered to be rather poor. I suppose the English rich always think they're poor. I decided to save all the money I could when I was twelve, after my mother said I couldn't ever go to school because she didn't believe in girls going. I collected pocket money and that sort of thing and wrote to Drummonds, which was our bank, saying here's ten shillings for my running-away account. And they wrote back saying 'Dear Madam, enclosed pass-book number so and so for your running-away account.' And then it signed off 'Your obedient servants Drummonds' and I thought that was exciting, so I kept saving.

JP It has been said that you were a left-wing duckling in a well-feathered nest. Could you describe the relationships with your parents and sisters and the political differences that set you apart?

JM It starts with the parents, I mean everything would. They were really just ordinary, extremely conservative people living in the country with a large family. In fact it was like two families: the first four children started with Nancy born in 1904 and then Pam,

Tom and Diana. Then there was a gap and I suppose my mother might have hoped that was the end, instead of which appeared Unity in 1914, me in 1917 and Debbo in 1920. Nancy was sort of the star of the family, indisputably so, and she started to write when she was about twenty-nine and she lived at home. Pam was a sort of country person, my brother Tom read law, and then came Diana who was another star. In those days we had beauties with a capital B and she was one of them. She married young, at eighteen to Brian Guinness, but left him to go off with Sir Oswald Mosley. Now we're into about 1933, when I was fifteen and Unity was eighteen; she got absolutely besotted with the fascists, became a member and went off to Germany where she met Hitler. I hated the whole idea and became a communist or said I was. I wasn't really a member, I don't think they took girls of fifteen, especially from Swinbrook. I suppose it was partly a reaction against what the others were doing, but not completely that. I was influenced by the whole generation that I grew up in and particularly by people who would have been twenty-five or thirty when I was fifteen and were involved in that tremendously political period of the 1930s. There was a huge lot of fascinating ideas swirling about outside Swinbrook which one picked up by reading. It's odd now to think about it but Unity and I were very close, we were each other's favourites. We were both outsiders from the grown-ups and we fought over issues. I mean we would start by slanging each other and then we'd start throwing things, and then Nanny used to come in and stop us. I wasn't helped by the fact that my parents went absolutely over for fascism, went to Germany and met Hitler. I found my mother's diaries after she died and it had things like 'in the middle of Nanny's holiday, calf born to a cow called Clover, tea with Fuehrer'.

JP   A few years ago Nicholas Mosley said that, in your ability to be impressed by orderliness and show you were not so very different from your sister Unity, the same family trait produced fascism and communism in two people.

JM   Oh now this point's been made by other people, this idea about two sides of the same coin. Well I completely reject that and I can't see any similarity no matter what you say. There is the disappointing failure of the countries that are born communist to produce true communism, but the motivation of people who go fascist or communist is totally different. And I don't think it's family traits at all. As I say, I think in my case it came far more from outside the family, that is, the influence of people just like Claud Cockburn, let's say, who was maybe half a generation older than I. And don't forget that, for instance, the Oxford Union pledged not to fight for king and country; oh that caused a stir the likes of which you can't believe. This was a time of real hunger, unemployment, fascism and so the loadstone for me was anything away from that, namely in those days, the Communist Party.

JP You eloped to Republican Spain; was that a romantic or a political decision?

JM Well it started off terribly political and then it sort of got romantic rather soon. What happened is that I knew all about Esmond Romilly who was a second cousin, and I'd read his book which he'd written when he was fifteen, called *Out of Bounds*, all about him running away from Wellington, and I'd followed his career in the newspapers. He was always being featured as Winston Churchill's red nephew and this sort of thing. So I sort of really rather fell in love with him from afar, I'd never met him, and when we did actually meet he'd just been invalided out of Spain where he was with the International Brigade. The first words I said were, 'Are you going back to Spain?' and he said, 'Yes,' and I said, 'Will you take me with you?' and he said 'Yes.' And it wasn't you know with any intention of romance, it was the idea that I wanted to get there and so he agreed but then once we were there, well you know, that's how things changed. We got married, later Esmond went to Canada to train for the war and during the middle of his training we had a daughter. About eight months after this he died.

JP After the war you re-married and became active in working and raising money for the Communist Party in America. There are some interesting stories from that period aren't there?

JM Well you see we were constantly trying to think of new ways of raising money and one thing we used to do in those days was to donate blood; you could get 25 dollars for a pint. So of course one kept sort of proliferating, I mean the ideas kept germinating as to what else you could do. By then they had this sort of semen bank, and I was thinking of the seaman's branch of the Communist Party which is, you know, self-explanatory, people who are sailors or trawler men, dockers and that kind of thing, and that this would be the perfect activity for them, to donate to the semen bank. But I was cautioned that the women's commission wouldn't like it because they'll be obviously excluded from this activity you see, and I suppose that is rather true. And we were told that you could get 75 dollars from medical schools for a corpse in good condition so I was thinking of getting every comrade to will his body to a medical school and get the money with the slogan: every contact a body, and the theme song would be 'Give a body, meet a body'.

JP Tell me about the incident when you talked your way out of a rape attack.

JM This was about 51 or 52 long before rape became fashionable; there weren't many cases of it. I was walking at night across a common and heard running steps behind me, looked round, and the fellow put his fingers round my mouth. I got one finger in my mouth and gave it a huge long bite but he still wrestled me down the hill into a culvert which couldn't be seen from the road. He said something like 'Oh, I haven't had a woman for a year and I've been in Korea,' and I said that was a pity but why didn't he get a nice girl of his own age and find a nice cosy bed – I didn't know if he was drunk or crazy or what. I thought if only I can keep talking and bore him stiff, or unstiff you might say. I said he ought to join the peace committee and did a rather mean thing, I gave him the name and phone number of the secretary of the committee who I didn't much like.

JP But behind the humour you were dedicated. Did the McCarthy witch-hunts get to you?

JM Yes, yes they did and it was an amazing time. You'd go off to work in the morning and there's an indistinct figure in the bushes who hands you a subpoena. I was secretary of the

Oakland Civil Rights Congress which meant I had custody of the records and the financial memberships and all that. They wanted me to hand these over; if I refused I was in contempt and could go to jail. The newspapers had everybody's photo on the front page and my daughter Dinky, Esmond Romilly's child, was teased about it at school. So I thought that I'd take her along to the hearing. I went to see her headmistress, who I was more frightened of than the committee, and she was marvellous, said Dinky should go so that if I did go to jail she would find out what the crime was I'd committed. Remember she was a state teacher, and could have been fired for that.

When I got to the hearing there were friends in the audience which made me feel a lot better. What you had to do was to take the Fifth Amendment which is a technical thing and consists of repeating to every question, 'I refuse to answer on the grounds that my answer would tend to incriminate me.' It's very boring after a while as they ask all the usual questions, member of the Communist Party? member of the Civil Rights Congress? And finally he said are you a member of the Berkely; I thought he said the Berkely Tenant's club. Well I knew tenants were subversive because they weren't landlords – it sort of figures. So I refused to answer. There was a roar of laughter; what he'd actually said was the Berkely Tennis club which is a posh conservative stronghold. At that point I was dismissed as being unresponsive.

JP   But you did get an FBI file didn't you?

JM   Yes, it was marvellous! It was 350 pages, not as many as some people had, but quite respectable. Most of it was blanked out, it would have 'subject seen entering' and then a huge blank. You have to pay 10 cents a page for these to be xeroxed so I'm appealing on the grounds that I shouldn't have to pay for the blanks. But it also listed lots of things that I'd forgotten about, in other words you see your whole life going by. There was also an X by the name of those to be held in case of trouble in a concentration camp. I was pleased to see that I was one of those listed. I'd have felt dreadful if I hadn't; in other words just been one of those considered not threatening enough to be put away.

JP   Why did you leave the Communist Party?

JM Well we were all committed to developing in California what we could in the way of a programme. First off we'd fight for civil rights and that sort of thing and of course leading to the ultimate goal of socialism. But after the Khrushchev Report came out about the crimes of Stalin a terrific number of people were totally disillusioned about the party. But I stayed, though it didn't mean that all of our principles had changed. Then came Hungary. In 1957 I was a delegate to one of the national conventions of the party in New York, and most of the group from California believed in an indigenous American road to socialism, working for things which were important to people in the country now. This idea seemed to win the convention but in the end the old-timers won and the party just became a tiny sect with no interest any more. It was all a huge waste of time while other things were happening, the civil rights movement had been taken over very largely by young college people and I sort of lurked away, without any animosity but because it seemed like a pointless endeavour.

In England and America the young get fired up by stories of those days and I remember one student saying we could still be doing things like that, that there were tremendous cases of injustice with mothers and welfare and so on. But even if you can help a specific case you must have a general theory, helping one mother is not going to advance humanity as a whole. It's very difficult.

JP You probably became most notorious in the United States for your book *The American Way of Death*, which had an enormous impact. What is the history of that book; why did you begin it?

JM Well actually my husband Bob was the one who got me on to it. He's a lawyer in Oakland and around about the middle 1950s he began to notice that trade unionists he represented were getting an extremely bad deal. When a breadwinner died the death benefits, which had been fought for by the unions through strikes, were supposed to go to the widow and family but instead would always end up in the pocket of an undertaker. If the death benefit was a 1,000 dollars that would be the price of the funeral, if it was 1,200 dollars the funeral would rise in cost as well. Bob started an organization which was a non-profit thing to reduce the high costs of funerals and I'm afraid I used to rather laugh at them and ask them about their lay-away plan. Then I saw the trade magazines, *Mortuary Management*, *Casket* and *Sunnyside* and my favourite title of all, *Concept, The Journal of Creative Ideas for Cemeteries*. Well I mean there was a whole wonderworld of the mortuary which I hadn't known existed. I hadn't known, for instance, that you could have a choice of foam-rubber or inner-spring mattress in your eternal sealer casket.

The entire story was very funny but the book did manage to change a few things. A lot of states changed their laws and then the Federal Trades Commission said that you had to list your goods and services and that sort of thing. Very mild, but the undertakers screamed with rage. I was sent on a tour of the whole country, sixteen cities or something, to promote the book. And as I went there was a package from the undertakers sent to the media and to radio stations which consisted of my entire communist record as told by the House UnAmerican Activities committee. I still get *Mortuary Management* and my name is in it, every copy; they call me Jessica, which I always think is the height of fame, like being called Za Za or Marilyn. And they seem to think that I invented cremations, because when I was writing the book the incidence of cremation in the populus as a whole was three per cent, it's now eleven per cent. Why it terrifies them is because unlike any other industry their market is inelastic, one to a customer. There was a terribly sad article in *Mortuary Management* saying that due to the national speed limit being reduced and due to medical advances in cancer and heart attacks, the death rate is falling. Terrible! I mean you can see their plight.

JP You saw the appeasement of the 1930s. How do you react now when people are accused of appeasing the Russians because they don't support the foreign policies of Reagan and Thatcher?

JM To me that's a lot of nonsense. The efforts to draw a parallel, which Mrs Thatcher and her people do, between appeasement of Hitler, Mussolini and Franco and what they call appeasement of the Russians is absurd. In the 1930s you have to remember that large sections of the English ruling class were incredibly in favour of that fella Hitler, as he was called in those days. Because what he'd done was crush the trade unions, he'd crushed the

Communist Party and he'd crushed the Jews. Don't forget there's a huge strain of anti-semitism that runs through that class in England. It makes you feel that a study of the origins of English fascism would go far beyond the absurdities of Sir Oswald Mosley.

I think the same strains are still here. Since the war with the immigration of black people there had been a large amount of absolutely unregenerate racialism that prevails at all levels and especially of course in the ruling class but it goes down to the working class too. Obviously some of the views of those at the top have modernized, a lot of them have lost their money so they can't have ten servants any more; but central, rock-bottom feelings haven't changed all that much I'm sure.

JP   When you come back to this country, as you do quite often, do you see more or fewer freedoms?

JM   Much fewer. You see when I first went to America I couldn't get a passport; in fact I never could get one. But in 1955 the state department issued one by mistake and they sent a telegram saying 'Passport issued by mistake, do not use under penalty of the law,' so we fled using it every inch of the way and came back to England for the first time. Now this was in the very height of what is loosely known as the McCarthy era in America, and England seemed a haven of liberty in every kind of way. It was just inconceivable to us, say, to walk into the offices of the *Daily Worker*, find them riding high and absolutely ordinary, and to meet people who were open communists. I mean it just wasn't happening in the United States.

It seems to me that there has been a total reversal with the two countries in a sense, because I'm told for instance by British journalists that the exposure of Watergate couldn't have happened in this country because of the Official Secrets Act and also the libel laws. Even if you had the goods on somebody like Nixon there would be no way of getting it printed for fear of those two things. I wrote a book about prisons in America. I'm told that over here journalists are forbidden to go into prisons at all except with special permission. There's no constitution, no bill of rights, there are no rights in England.

JP You've been closely connected with the black struggles in the United States. Can you tell me about your civil rights work?

JM In 1951 William McGee, a black worker in a town called Laurel in Mississippi, was accused of raping a white woman. Now the evidence in the case was that he'd been having an affair with her, really at her insistence, for several years and when her husband looked as though he was finding out she said that McGee had raped her. It was the death penalty you know for any black to rape a white person so this became an international issue. A lot of men had been down, lawyers and journalists, and they'd been beaten up, so we organized a women's delegation from Oakland and rather assumed there would be hundreds there. It turned out that we were the only ones; it was rather dreary. So we checked into the YMCA, which we thought would be safe, and every morning we'd set out with hats, gloves and stockings – and we'd be sure that our stocking seams were straight, a great preoccupation in those days. The point was, we looked like southern ladies.

We went from door to door speaking about the case but needless to say it wasn't long before the police caught on and there was a huge headline in the Jackson and Mississippi newspaper saying 150 women were campaigning for the life of William McGee; there were only four of us so we were rather proud as you can imagine. We were evicted from the Y and found lodgings on the outskirts of town for a dollar a night. People were so pleased to get the dollar that they really didn't mind what we were there for. The response from most people was terrible: you know, they should have burned him the day it happened sort of thing.

But we did begin to get somewhere and got some support from white people, but nobody wanted their names mentioned in any context. I had the idea to try to get a famous person to come on our side. The only person who was famous in Mississippi was Faulkner, so we drove to Oxford and asked a sort of gangling white boy, 'Where is Mr Faulkner's house?' and he said, 'It's down the road apiece past the weeping willow tree,' and I knew I was in Faulkner country. We went in without an appointment and he spoke for two hours with me trying to write it all down. The Civil Rights Congress in New York were thrilled but said I would have to get him to initial it or he might repudiate it later when the pressure was on. So I went back and there he was in a typical Faulkner attitude up to his hips in muck in a pair of dungarees. I showed him the statement and he signed it, and then said, 'I think they should both be destroyed,' meaning McGee and his white mistress, so I said thanks and ran back to my car as quickly as I could. William McGee was executed; it was an incredible case.

JP   Is it possible to compare the racial situation in America to that of Britain, because there are people here who've had a pretty high-tone view of this country and its attitudes, isn't that right?

JM   High-tone and extremely smug, with no understanding of what was involved. When we first came back here there was an advertisement in the underground for Idris, and it showed a disgusting-looking sort of huge fat-lipped black person sucking a water-melon and the slogan said 'When eyes dry Idris' or something like that. And we were appalled; I mean in America even in the 1950s there would have been such a howl of protest about anything of that sort. So when we said this to English friends, English left-wing friends, let's say communist friends, they'd say it was just a joke and that there was no discrimination in England. The next time we came over here was when those Notting Hill riots took place and the whites were on a rampage led by Sir Oswald Mosley's children, killing and beating.

There are some major similarities between the States and here. One that meets the eye is that blacks are relegated to the lowest kinds of jobs, even when they have good qualifications. What is missing here is the great protest that took place in America in the sixties when both black and white people campaigned. And here it hasn't really happened partly perhaps because the percentages are so different. We've got something between ten and twenty per cent depending on where you are, here it's something like three per cent. So in other works they haven't much political clout. The liberals don't help and Labour doesn't do much because they're as racist as anybody. And we've talked to black people, and that's what they'll tell you in England.

6 David Williamson

The artistic revolution in Australia in the late 1960s and early 1970s produced a host of young people intent on either presenting, explaining or destroying the antipodean caricature. One such is David Williamson, generally considered to be his country's finest playwright and most successful screen-writer. While contemporaries have often been prepared to pander to the beliefs of London and Sydney theatre-goers, Williamson has employed an acute honesty and balanced judgement in his work, gaining him international prestige and a collection of awards.

He was born in 1942 in Melbourne, studied for a degree in structural engineering at university, then lectured for a time before turning to full-time writing. His first success was *The Removalists* which transferred from the Nimrod Theatre, Sydney, to the Royal Court and New York. It deals with a station sergeant and a recruit helping an attractive girl to move her furniture without her husband finding out. The themes are violence, male attitudes towards women and other men and the issue of role playing – recurring subjects in Williamson's writing. For the Royal Court production the then *Evening Standard* named him 'Most Promising Playwright'. Two years later the Court was once again the venue for his next major piece, *Don's Party*. This time the setting was a drinks party in an Australian city with alcohol and recriminations flowing. It was well received by British audiences, more so than his most recent London play, *The Perfectionist*, at the Hampstead Theatre.

Time Out drama critic Steve Grant sees Williamson as 'the first writer to realistically depict Australian life to the English. We'd had Barry Humphries being very funny and we all assumed we knew about Sydney and Melbourne, but we didn't. He's very strong on dialogue, has an understanding of character and generally gets his points across well. Not that the material is presented in a particularly radical manner, he still uses the well-made play, but he's made an impression on a lot of people. I finally understood the pressures of living out there, realized that there is a fear of sensitivity and hence a willingness to label people as homosexual or communist as a sort of defence mechanism.'

Williamson is now concentrating on film writing. In *Gallipoli* he attempted to show the stupidity and callousness of the British establishment during the First World War. Whatever the work may have lacked in casting or direction it made up for in a long-overdue and, at times, bitter explosion of an imperial myth for which many Australian soldiers had been sacrificed. His last film, *The Year of Living Dangerously*, told of a cynical war reporter caught up in a romance and a lead story. His screen adaptations of his own plays have tended to be more successful, retaining the craft and humour of the stage.

He is a large man with expressive hands and a subdued way of recounting anecdotes. His wife, Kristin, is a journalist and, between them, including previous marriages, they have four children. Apart from a short spell when he accepted a visiting professorship of dramatic writing at the Danish University of Aarhus, he now spends all his time as a writer. When asked to comment on the rather black, dry wit which permeates his material, Williamson pauses, laughs to himself and tells a joke: 'A drunk in Melbourne sits on a bench, sees a man tie a length of rope to a tree, put a noose around his neck and jump. "Stupid bastard," says the drunk, "made the rope too long and only broke his leg." '

JP David, you once said that your mother had to apologize to her local bowls club for your filthy plays. Does she still have to?

DW No, I think a few of the later ones have got less obscene and a few of the films have been quite polite so it's OK now. It's a bit worrying, if I'm okay at the local bowls club maybe I've lost my cutting edge. But people's reactions had more to do with the subject matter of my work than the language. Australia is a much more aggressive, acquisitive society than this country, and the class barriers are much more fluid. So there's more point in striving to improve oneself; whereas in Britain everyone seems to be a lot happier slotted into their own class levels, they don't worry. Within one's lifetime, in Sydney in particular, your status is shown by accumulation of goods, the house you live in and your ostentation. I've written about that in my plays; that's sometimes upset people.

In Australia we're still influenced by our origins, still have some colonial hangovers. Not so much with the convict roots of people but the massive working-class migration from the British Isles that happened around the gold-rush time; they brought with them tribal working-class values like respectability, conformity and anything that would make you fit into a developing industrial machine. These values have transmuted three generations. But the one positive aspect of it all, the tribal support part, has been lost. We're left with a ridiculous concern for suburban neatness and the ethos of the nuclear family.

The statement that Australia is a working-class paradise with a middle-class veneer has some truth in it. Bob Hawke said a couple of years ago that there are two classes in the country, the employed and the unemployed. The unemployed are really badly off; anyone who has a job is comparatively well off. The spread of income is more even than any country in the world I believe, so the egalitarian myth is not quite a myth, there's a basis of truth in the fact that a blue-collar worker gets just as much if not more than a white-collar worker if he's in a skilled trade.

We still agonize over our identity, and those who do the agonizing come from the intellectual, artistic portion of Australian society who are very worried about the fact that they haven't got an artistic history. Because part of anyone's self-esteem comes from the artistic achievement of one's own society. I mean you've only got to look at the French; their incredible arrogance derives from the very substantial artistic history of France, so every Frenchman can claim to be part of that. Australia hasn't got its impressionist painters, hasn't got its William Shakespeare; it makes people desperately worried. Until recently universities teaching English literature weren't allowed to study Australian writers. We were told that there were only five great prose writers in the world and they were all English, so kids found themselves disenfranchized from their own culture and became totally orientated towards England; and over 200 years the cultures have become quite distinct and quite unique.

JP   What are the differences?

DW   Well we've already touched on them. Australia is a much more cynical and deeply ironic country at base because it evolved in the way it did. It's always assumed for instance that public office is for private gain, the ethical sense of the British tradition has never really figured in the Australian psyche. During the Watergate crisis the Australian attitude was that you expect politicians to do that, he was unlucky to get caught and of course he had to step down. But it was a pragmatic rather than a moralistic and earnest reaction. There have been stories circulating for the last ten years about the behaviour of various top politicians and their connections with organized crime, they're commonplace gossip in Australia. I don't think idealism is a very deep-rooted impulse in our society and never has been, because of the nature of the way the country started. Life was against you from the beginning and if you could make something of yourself by fair means or foul, good luck to you.

You can also contrast Australian attitudes to those in America. Superficially the two countries have got similar cultures, but because of America's petty-bourgeois origins they always think success means superior inner qualities and a successful person is enterprising and bold. If success happens to an Australian it's because he's devious or a criminal or sycophantic, and that's still the underlying assumption. It's the tall-puppy syndrome, that if you do any good you're knocked down because you haven't got there through positive qualities. Australia is still searching for an identity, and that does make it difficult and confusing for young Australians. They know they're different from British, they're not always sure why.

JP Gallipoli has always played an important part in the Australian mind, as has the Second World War. There are certain paradoxes there, aren't there?

DW Yes, because however heroic Gallipoli may have been it was still a military failure. Australia was for a long time represented by its soldiers and sportsmen, and during the first war the way to maintain national self-esteem was to link yourself very closely to England, which still had huge international prestige at the turn of the century. If we could become one of the good children of the motherland we would be respected. And that trend persisted for a long time; as late as the fifties Sir Robert Menzies was still stating that we are British to our bootstraps. But as England's international esteem took a downhill slope, attaching yourself to the mother country didn't seem a viable strategy any more. We had finally to do something ourselves.

I'm working on a television series called 'The Last Bastion' which looks at the central issues of this relationship; when, between January and June of 1942, the Japanese were advancing south at a very rapid rate and it looked athough they had definite invasion plans for Australia. The country was caught totally unawares, it was still working under the Imperial Defence Policy under which the colonies sent troops to help the motherland when it was threatened and England would send aid to the colonies if they were in trouble. Australian troops were in the Middle East fighting under Churchill's command, but he was very reluctant to let them get back to Australia even though the country was under severe threat.

Churchill did eventually agree to let the troops come home from the Middle East but at the last minute he diverted them to Burma, which he thought was a much more strategic battle-ground at that time. The Australian Prime Minister found himself in a position of not really being in command of his own Australian army. Churchill was so sure that Australia would not dare defy him. What did happen in the end is that although the Japanese navy was dead keen to put ten divisions ashore just north of Sydney the army was more cautious, and finally on 15 March the army won. But Australia wasn't being hysterical, the fears were well-grounded and she had virtually no trained men with which to defend herself at that time. Churchill felt Burma was more important because India was a jewel in the empire's crown, so Australia found that this so-called Imperial Defence Policy really meant we help the motherland full stop.

We didn't have an independent foreign policy, separate from the States and from Britain, until the 1970s when the Whitlam government made a stab at it. The old ideas were prolonged by political figures like Bob Menzies who kept insisting on bringing royal visitors out and trooping school-children out to wave British flags. I can remember at the age of about seven or ten or something being assembled with two million other school-children and taken on trains from all over to a cricket ground where we were meant to be struck down with charismatic awe at the sight of two specks in an open Rolls Royce three miles away. It was ludicrous the extent to which our leaders like Bob Menzies tried to maintain this fervent loyalty to England by these devices, and obviously England wanted to maintain them too or they wouldn't have sent these specks in Rolls Royces to our country. Even when I was seven I couldn't quite understand why, when this queen in this far-off land had a baby, we were all given a holiday.

The shadow has been diminishing for a long while, I mean there's not much of a shadow to stand in if I can be blunt and rude. When Di and Charles came over the fervour was much less than when I was a kid in the fifties. The numbers were the same as if a television star came over from America, although the British press were frantically trying to promote this picture of antipodean loyalty to Charles and Di and there were triumphant comments about 3,000 people lining the main streets and so much for Bob Hawke's republicanism. I couldn't believe it; yes there were a few children there and there might have been some bowls ladies, but I'm sure that was provoked by human interest in two characters who get a lot of press coverage rather than loyalty to the future king of England. Middle-aged, middle Australia is still torn, but there's no doubt among young Australians that royalty is an anachronism.

What there is in Australia is a fear of someone from the north, a yellow peril. Consequently for a long time we looked for some form of patron. You see we see ourselves as very desirable in our rich, not heavily populated country and America is the obvious choice for a protector; Britain was until World War Two but I don't think there's any sense that the British fleet will come and rescue us anymore. The Falklands for example was seen as a type of World Cup soccer match, as a rather imbecilic exercise in old-fashioned chauvinism on both sides. We couldn't identify with the Argentinians but on the other hand we couldn't pretend that Margaret Thatcher's England was behaving in a totally honourable way. One thing we still have in our psyche is that finally Britain is a moral country and it sticks to the rules. When it set that 200 mile limit around the island and sunk the *Belgrano* outside it a lot of us were shocked. It was deeply distressing. If anything the Falklands broadened the gap between Britain and Australia.

JP   There's a line in your play *The Perfectionist* where a middle-aged actress says that in her day she had to go to London to prove herself. Is that still true?

DW No I don't think so. There's a very definite feeling that we're a distinct English-speaking culture and that we really need to explore in our own way. A performer or film director can still transfer but Australian writers realize that they have to be on about what they know, and the playwrights who left and went to Britain in the fifties frankly didn't prosper creatively. After that wave there has been a feeling that fleeing is no solution for a creative artist. There is still what's been termed the cultural fringe; Australians don't always trust their own artistic judgement and so they wait for some kind of confirmation from overseas, but that's no different from America as late as the 1920s; they still regarded themselves as a colonial culture artistically and still felt ultimately inferior. I do think that any writer who leaves his country is in big trouble, big trouble. The impetus leaves them once they cut off their roots.

What can happen is that Australians come to Britain and try to become part of the literary establishment, but that's only a solution if you view Australia as a totally materialistic country which is anti-intellectual and anti-creative. I don't view the country that way. It's an exciting place to be in creatively because we haven't exhausted all the artistic traditions, we're onto the first stepping stones of creating an artistic culture. The other view is to forget that you're an Australian and knock off all those bad edges and become part of the larger English-speaking world in Britain and America. That rarely succeeds, people don't realize how different the cultures are at a very deep level. You need a lifetime to learn about the subtler differences between the apparently similar English-speaking countries, and all good New York writers or Southern writers for example operate out of their knowledge of New York or the South. Culture is very hard to learn, you can't pick it up overnight.

JP You've made a reputation in the film industry as a writer, as an Australian writer. Could you explain about the new Australian cinema and the change in attitudes?

DW   It's all tied up with Australian art and its implications. We certainly haven't got a wealth of deeply tragic 'national catastrophe' type stories; we haven't had our population decimated like in Russia, we haven't had a civil war like in America. But we still have the basic elements, we still love and hate, we're still rejected and feel loss or anger. I think artistically it took us a while to realize that we were worthy and human and had the sort of emotions that feed into fiction. Nowadays Australia does want cultural heroes but it's what Thomas Keneally described as premature canonization: you're treated like a saint after your first artistic success and then you spend the rest of your life drinking in bars because you're not Dostoyevsky.

All this applies to the cinema in Australia; we've found the motivation and the reasons but we haven't found all the answers yet. Sydney has become the focus of deals and projects and it does have that Los Angeles feel about it at the moment because the government tax concessions are generous and they're promoting investment in films. So producers are desperately getting packages together which will be saleable to investors, and there is a danger that with fifty features made a year a country of fifteen million people may not have the talent and imagination to maintain the standard.

There's also a feeling of tribal loyalty, that if directors go abroad they've somehow let the side down. Bruce Beresford went to America and has made what you can only describe as American films, but perhaps he brought an Australian sensibility or work method to them. He hasn't come in for too much criticism. The same can't be said about Fred Schepisi and his film *The Chant of Jimmie Blacksmith*; he came in for a lot of attack because that film was just too honest for the Australian psyche at that particular point in time . He depicted the extreme racism and also described the Aboriginals as living in squalor – as they do. Fred was criticized on both sides, the Aboriginals hated the film and so did the white establishment. And that was very wounding, because he knew and a lot of us knew that it was a very good movie.

JP   Could that have had more to do with Australian racial attitudes than with artistic content?

DW   Yes, very possibly. It goes back to the feelings brought to Australia by the early immigrants, there's no doubt that they were influenced by the nineteenth-century colonial-master mentality. The treatment of the indigenous people was appalling, but no more appalling than any other white nation at that time in history. I don't think Australians have got to feel a special sense of guilt that they were in some way more hideous than other people; we haven't after all made 5,000 films like John Wayne Westerns showing the natives as being sub-human. But there's certainly a deep sense of guilt; whenever there's a referendum on whether Aboriginal conditions should be improved the vote is ninety-six per cent. Amongst writers and artists there's a feeling that the Aboriginals themselves can more truthfully tell their own story. I don't know whether that's justified or not but it's the same as a man trying to write a women's liberationist play. I don't feel I should personally suffer because of the prevailing ideology that my great, great grandfather brought to the country.

More recently Australia has changed racially, with less and less of the English component. Now the traditional thing to say is that this has been an enormously invigorating event for our society, to have all these different people opening restaurants and everything. There are some fears that minor populations have assimilated so well that perhaps we're not getting the spin-off that we should be getting from the cultural tension. It's been remarked that the Greek taxi drivers seem to be more Australian in their accents and attitudes than Australians themselves. There's been a lot of tension recently between the Vietnamese and the white Australian working class who are living in the same areas. It's the first serious episode of contemporary racism that we've had for a long while. Even though the Italian and Greek communities do tend to live in certain areas there seems to be a high aspiration on their part to assimilate into the major culture. In fact it's difficult to draw any realistic conclusions.

JP   But there's also a new Australia in other ways isn't there?

DW   There has been for some time, and in literature it's been an enduring theme. The early settlers tried to turn a vast, frightening land into part of Europe with green lawns and houses neat and warm. As recently as twenty years ago people were still wearing serge suits in the middle of summer, whereas today the summer means beach time. The Barry Humphries caricature has developed, the vulgarity and the humour; we recognize a lot of that, realize that we haven't always made advances in the right direction. What has been very important is the growth of the republican movement, the feeling that the British and Australian cultures are so disparate in their aims and life-styles that it would be foolish for Australia not to be a republic. We'd have control of our own destiny in a psychological sense, the highest court of appeal would be Australian, there'd be no dismissal of governments by the Queen's appointees. We have to acknowledge that we are now a very different country from the country our forefathers left 200 years ago.

7 Salman Rushdie

Best-selling author Salman Rushdie is a man of paradoxes. Although an insider – he received a privileged education, has never been less than comfortable and in 1981 won the Booker McConnell Prize for Fiction – he was born a Muslim in India, lived for a time as an Indian in Pakistan with his family, and is now an Asian residing in Britain.

His birthplace was Bombay in 1945 and after primary education in India he was sent to Rugby School. As a history student at King's College, Cambridge, he took part in the 'Footlights' revue, acted on the fringe after he came down and finally settled for a short-term career as a copy-writer. It was during this period that he wrote *Midnight's Children*. His first book, *Grimus*, had appeared in 1975 and, though not a failure, was dismissed by the majority of critics. *Midnight's Children* won praise and acclaim from almost every section of the literary community, achieved ecstatic reviews and did well with the book-buying public.

It's a mammoth volume which took four years to write and the large scope of the work has caused problems of definition. As well as being a political novel (there is a skilfully constructed attack on the regime of Mrs Gandhi), it displays a combination of comedy and narrative which makes it much more than another work of social fiction. The use of language, possibly drawn from Rushdie's Indian background, and ambitious range of the book, turned its author into a new discovery.

Two years later he published *Shame*, a tighter work and scathing in its condemnation of Pakistani politics and government. Once again he employed clever and well-thought-out techniques, resulting in a novel which angered the ruling powers in Islamabad. Rushdie's editor at Jonathan Cape, Liz Calder, says of him, 'His quality as a story-teller is remarkable, he can't resist a good tale and has an unbounded delight in passing it on. Technically he's in a class of his own, using language in a daring and exciting way, weaving plots with verve; never were so many balls in the air brought to earth with such panache. The characters are quite simply people I'd love to meet, people who seem familiar but at the same time existing in a political and social background which is always a revelation. And he's very, very funny.'

He is a likeable, unpretentious and highly articulate man, with a penchant for stylish hats and an ability to make dated anecdotes seem fresh. Outside the literary world he has worked within the Asian community to improve and reform race relations. When broadcasting on television, as in the following Channel 4 'Opinions' piece, he never pulls any punches: 'The ease with which the English language allows the terms of racial abuse to be coined: wog, frog, kraut, dago, spic, yid, coon, nigger, Argie. Can there be another language with so wide-ranging a vocabulary of racist denigration?'

Salman Rushdie is now part of an artistic elite, but it's not so much this which distinguishes him, rather it is a combination of radical intent and an uncompromising belief in his origins and talent.

JP   Could you describe your own childhood, the economic condi-tions you grew up in, the contrasts that were before you?

SR   I grew up in a very affluent family. They weren't one of the super-rich of Bombay, richer than whom or more super than whom there are no rich, but we were well off. And so one of the things that happens is that you grow up with servants which is something with which English people are no longer really familiar. I was brought up by servants, not by my parents, and spent a lot of time with my ayah or nanny so in a way I was given access to worlds a comparable English upper-middle-class child would not be able to get into. For instance, the same thing happened to Kipling because when Kipling was growing up in India he was also brought up by the servants to the extent that he spoke Hindi as a first language, and when he was shown in to his parents at the cocktail hour or at tea-time his ayah would have to remind him to speak to them in English. It's quite valuable in retrospect because it means that if I want to write about a poor person in Bombay I actually have material to do it with.

When I went to Rugby I was made to feel an outsider which is odd because I would have thought I was perfect public school material: kind of upper-middle-class, recently colonial, quite kind of snobbish because that was in the air. The idea that one was not high Tory had not occurred to me. And Rugby in a sort of way did me a favour because it cured me of all that. Not because of the staff, because the education was extraordinary and I was better taught at Rugby than I was ever taught before or since and much better than I was taught at university, although it helped that there were kind of five or six children to a class. The problem came from the children who very rapidly demonstrated to me that whatever I thought, whether I thought that I belonged to this society or not, they were not going to permit me to belong and that I wasn't one of them and there was really no point in me trying to be.

They expressed their attitudes by a series of little persecutions I suppose. I'd find essays that I'd written torn up and left in pieces on the floor of the room or things written up on the wall. I did actually do at this point my most violent act, which is sort of connected to the character in *Shame* who becomes violent. I got into my room, one of these little cubby holes for all studies which you shared with two other boys, and I discovered one of the other boys who was about fourteen and a half, I suppose, like me, writing 'Wogs go home' on the wall and he still had the crayon in his hand so he couldn't deny that it was him. So I remonstrated with him, let us say, told him that this was not a good thing to do. And he became brazen and said so what and that I deserved it. I went crazy really, got into a fit where I was possessed by this anger and I attacked him. Or this anger inside me attacked him. I did something which was very strong and I wasn't then or now particularly physically strong – I grabbed him by the seat of his pants with my right hand and by the collar of his shirt with my left hand and I swung him off the ground and rammed him head first into the wall, head first into the 'Wogs' of 'Wogs go home'. And he passed out on the floor of the study and I thought I'd killed him, started doing B-movie things like pouring water on him. I knew what wogs meant and I found it rather appalling that it meant me. The idea of myself as a foreigner was completely alien to me but suddenly I was foreign, and also a racially inferior foreigner.

JP What was the purpose of writing your two books about the sub-continent?

SR Well it's changed really. With *Midnight's Children* there was a purpose which pre-dated the plot, which was that I had never read or couldn't remember reading a book about India in English that felt anything like the place that I'd known. So I thought that I wanted just to write a book that felt right, that would be an authentically felt experience about India from the inside, because so many of the books seemed to be about what happened to the West when it went East and I was interested in the other ninety-nine per cent. After that I began to feel that there was some unfinished business and stories to tell. One of those was the political relationship between Zia ul Haq and Mr Bhutto; Zia was a nobody who was picked out of obscurity to be Commander-in-Chief on the grounds that he was the most stupid man available. We all know what happened.

JP   Reading and watching you, you seem to be saying that although you've won the Booker Prize you're still seen as an immigrant, still the object of racism.

SR   Oh yes, that's something which is self-evidently true. All I can do is to occupy the time-honoured role of the uppity nigger. I mean I don't have any intention of denying my race, the fact that I'm fair-skinned and could therefore on some occasions pass for white makes me even more determined not to really. I'm not on the receiving end of racism very often but that's to do with class. I don't live on a council estate so I'm more cocooned from the storm.

    But I do believe that one of the most disturbing aspects of British politics is the way in which the establishment excuses people for holding certain kinds of views. I don't mean that people in high positions of power are closely connected with small ultra-ist groups because I don't think they are very likely, but there is a way in which they can create the atmosphere of a society and they can excuse these groups their views. Sometimes it's a little more direct than that. I recall shortly after the disturbances in Southall in which Blair Peach died, the Community Relations Committee in Camden, where I live, wanted to hold a meeting to discuss the events. So a meeting was set up and the hall was found and apparently the same hall had been attacked by the National Front during a similar meeting a couple of years before. We were worried and went to see the police and asked for some police protection, and the police refused. Why? Because this meeting should not be held because the issue was not a Camden issue and we had no business discussing police practice in another area. The obvious point to make is that if that had been a National Front meeting the police would have protected it. Not only that, a letter was written to each member of Camden Council recommending that they look at the activities of the local community relations committee with a view to penalizing them financially. The police, when it suits them, drop all that rhetoric about freedom of speech.

JP   Is this kind of thing allowed to happen because there is no facing of the facts on a national basis? For example, when the 1981 Nationality Act went through the most important thing was the the right to call yourself British if you were born here was taken away.

SR   That's right, it's appalling because it seems that that was an issue so much huger than the kind of racial dimension, it affected every person who was likely to have a child born in this country though of course it wasn't presented in that way. There was this thing called the law of the soil which had been in existence for nine centuries and which meant that whoever you were, whether you were illegal migrants or whatever, if you were born in England your parents' status was irrelevant and you were automatically a subject of the country. That had been a law which was not bad, it hadn't been shown to malfunction, and it was a right of each individual and not really in the gift of the government. The Nationality Act withdrew one of our fundamental rights, and this is nothing to do with whether one is white or black or green, it's to do with a right which had existed for 900 years. Now it went through on the nod more or less, with a few largely black groups protesting but as far as everyone else was concerned nothing particularly big was going on. It was presented in an innocuous way, saying that this was a way of keeping unacceptable people out of the country; as a racist law on the basis that we don't want floods of Kenyan Asians and citizens of Hong Kong and Singapore and let's not forget the Falkland Islands, who are also removed from British citizenship by the British Nationality Act. I gather one of the concessions that was made was when groupings of Tory females went to see Mrs Thatcher worrying about their daughters marrying South African businessmen; exemptions were made as a result.

JP What do you like about this country?

SR I enjoy lots of things about England apart from the fact that I have to sleep under blankets. But the Englands that I enjoy are at present not the ones that are in charge. I respect many things about the British intellectual tradition and English literature. I have lots of friends here, there are political Englands with which I feel in tune. There are all sorts of things to enjoy because you choose those bits of the country that you like to belong to – it's sad that those bits are currently in retreat. I don't myself think that that retreat is anything like as irreversible and final as one is led to believe. One of the characteristics of England is that when there's a swing to the right this is seen as being irreversible, and when there's a swing to the left this is only temporary.

JP Where are the great works of fiction presenting new ideas, where are the Orwells of race if you like?

SR Yes, exactly. Anyway there were never that many Orwells you know, I mean there was Orwell. There's no doubt that there has been a lull in the British novel, a reluctance to confront the central issues of society. I think the answer to your question is to go to the theatre; the theatre of this country in the last twenty years has been arguing very fiercely about the nature of Britain. There's been a generation, if not two, of writers of great quality who have been discussing these issues; I mean Hare, Griffiths and Brenton.

JP You began as an actor, didn't you?

SR That's a glorified thing to say. What I did at Cambridge was to act a lot more than anything else and when I left Cambridge I went on for a while on the fringe of Kennington in the Oval House. Really I acted in order to discover that I couldn't act. It was a very exciting time on the fringe then because there were all these people who are now household names just starting upstairs in pubs, so all around you there were people of considerable ability and what was clear was that I wasn't as good as them. So I stopped after about a year and because I didn't have any money got a job.

I'm afraid the enemies of promise drew me to advertising. What happened was that a friend, who shall be nameless but who is now quite a well-known playwright, got a job with J. Walter Thompson and he rang me up and suggested I try it because it was easy and paid lots of money. I went along and got what they call a 'copy test', which I failed. It was the last exam I ever did, lasted for three hours during which you wrote ads under exam conditions. One of the questions, and I've never forgotten it, said imagine that you meet a Martian who can speak English but who doesn't know what bread it, tell him in not more than twenty words how to make a piece of toast. I completely failed. Eventually I got a much more menial job at another advertising agency and got an arrangement where I did only a couple of days a week. I couldn't think of another way that I could get four days a week to sit at home and write, paid for by two days' work. That's how I wrote *Midnight's Children*, with a sort of industrial sponsorship.

JP   Your latest book *Shame* was a savage attack on the military hierarchy in Pakistan. Where did that anger come from?

SR   Although it looks like a savage attack what it actually is is a mild understatement of the nature of reality in Pakistan. You can't say the real stuff because nobody would believe it. How do you explain that there is a country which has become the world's largest exporter of heroin while at the same time returning to religious principles of a very extreme kind, and one of the justifications that is advanced for this is that the Koran does not ban heroin. It bans booze, so you can't drink a glass of beer and it closed down a couple of very good breweries that were there, but there are large numbers of soldiers making a killing out of heroin with the help of some of the richer of the Afghan refugees.

JP   When *Midnight's Children* was published you were a celebrity almost overnight. What were the side-effects of this instant fame?

SR   You mean apart from money? Well you get invited to free lunches, get to travel and you do meet famous people like politicians. I was invited to meet Mrs Gandhi shortly after *Midnight's Children* came out, I thought it was a hoax. Even Margaret Thatcher's government must know that you don't invite me to meet Indira Gandhi because I'd been very rude about her. I told them I couldn't come and it became clear that they didn't know anything about the content of *Midnight's Children*, and they blustered, got very flustered and said it was the Foreign Office that asked you, and you'd think they'd have read your book wouldn't you? They said they would ring me back and in the meanwhile I decided that I wouldn't go anyway, but I was longing for them to ring back and withdraw the invitation because they'd have looked like such fools. However they knew that they would look like fools so they rang back rather gracelessly and said why didn't I come anyway. To their great relief I backed out, and I thought that was the end of the story.

Not so. This lunch happened, and the next day Mrs Gandhi and Mrs Thatcher were at some function at which Mrs Thatcher made a speech about the historical relationship between India and Britain and in the middle of this speech she started talking about *Midnight's Children*, which clearly she hadn't read, but which she nevertheless praised highly. Mrs Gandhi sat there next to her sort of hatchet-faced, and then to complete it Mrs Thatcher turned to Mrs Gandhi and said, of course this is the book written by the man you met at lunch yesterday. History does not reveal her response.

8 Costa Gavras

There is something strangely apposite about Constantin Costa Gavras being born in 1933, the same year that Adolf Hitler finally came to power in Germany. Ever since he began to work in the film industry Gavras has made it his task to deflate and expose political authoritarianism in all its aspects.

He was brought up in Athens and came from a humble background with a peasant mother and a radical father of Russian origin. He found the archaic and often stagnant atmosphere of Greece unfulfilling and at nineteen travelled to Paris to study for a literature degree at the Sorbonne. He soon became tired of the dryness of the subject, looked to the cinema as an alternative, and enrolled at l'Institut des Hautes Etudes Cinématographiques. He went on to work as assistant to the highly respected directors René Clair, Yves Allegret, René Clement and Jacques Demy. In 1964 he made his own movie, *Sleeping Car Murders*, a Hitchcockian thriller. This was followed five years later by *One Man Too Many*, a work which explored the role of the French Underground in the Second World War.

It was not until 1969 that Gavras made an international impact and established his reputation as a director. The film was *Z*, the story of the assassination in 1963 of Gregorios Lambrakis, a left-wing political leader. It was a powerful indictment of the fascist regime in Greece, combining forthright statements with bitter humour, and demanding a first-class performance from its star Yves Montand. It received an Academy Award as best foreign film and gave fresh opportunities to its director.

The next year Gavras again shocked audiences, this time by showing the methods of Stalinist governments in forcing confessions from innocent victims. *The Confession* is set in Czechoslovakia and tells the story of the imprisonment, torture and trial of communist politician Artur London. It was important not just as a convincing portrayal of a confused man subjected to organized violence, but as a work of art breaking the taboo that the Soviet Union was not to be criticized by the Left. *The Confession* led to threats and attacks on Costa Gavras, culminating in widespread condemnation from Communist parties all over the world.

There followed two films in fairly quick succession, one dealing with the Vichy government's collaboration with the Nazis and the other, *State of Siege*, with the Tupamaros and the subject of terrorism in Uruguay. After rejecting *The Godfather* because of its weak attitude towards the Mafia and the drug trade, Gavras at first turned down *Missing* due to a love story which Hollywood intended to put into the film. He finally convinced them to leave it out, and this English-language film with Jack Lemmon and Sissy Spacek won critical acclaim. It is based on the book by Thomas Hauser and concerns the search by an American citizen for his son, a victim of Chilean fascists during the overthrow of President Allende.

His latest film, *Hannah K*, is set in Israel, and deals with the Palestinian issue and again with the subject of terrorism. The work has received limited distribution, possibly due to support for Israel inside the cinema industry, and mixed reviews. For Gavras, however, the response of the critic is not of paramount importance; he stresses the point that he is a man and a film-maker of the people, not a member of any elite. Indeed this shy man dismisses any film as 'a short moment, a song or a scream', stating that 'If you think a movie can change things you are misguided, it's insane to think a movie can change the world.' Perhaps this is true. But if any director's work is the exception it is his.

JP   Could you explain about your childhood and years as a student?

CG   Yes, my mother was very religious, my father wasn't, and she used to oblige us when we were young to go to the church on Sundays; and the Orthodox ceremony lasts two-and-a-half hours in ancient Greek, which nobody understood. I lost any sense of religion very soon, not as a reaction against my mother because I loved her very much and she was an important lady who pushed us to study and learn languages. Our family was poor, especially after my father lost his job. He was in the resistance with the anti-royalists, and when the King came back all the old anti-royalists lost their jobs and were sent off to prison on the islands. My father went to jail many times, many times. He was and still is a democrat, he opposed the foreign wars of the royal family and a lot of what they stood for. But those years were good ones for me. I remember going to the jail to bring food to my father and the only bad thing was seeing him in prison, but the other prisoners didn't have bad faces like killers or thieves, they were good people like my father.

After I left high school I couldn't go to university in Greece because of my father's politics, at that time you needed a kind of certificate to show that neither of your parents had been communists. It's funny because Milos Forman told me years later that in Czechoslovakia to go to university you had to bring a certificate showing that your parents had been communists. My mother told me to study abroad, I worked for a year, saved some money and then went to Paris. In France the students don't pay and you can eat and live for a limited amount, so I was able to go to the Sorbonne. After a while I felt very bored, it was all so static, and then I discovered the Institute for Cinema Studies. Being Greek didn't mean too much at that time, it was really after the colonels took over in 1967 that I felt passionately about my roots.

JP   Was it that feeling which provoked you make Z?

CG   Completely, made in passion and anger and much else. A Polish colleague told me that the film was seen as a lesson in his country because of its passion, that's probably the biggest compliment anybody has paid to Z. We spent a year and a half, maybe two years looking for money but everybody refused for various reasons. Show-business people used to say that there was no love story, put some love in it involving a woman and that might be different. Others said it was a political movie and audiences don't care about political movies. Every kind of reason. Then the Algerians gave us facilities, some crew and a place to stay; and part of the money came from a French distributor and the French state. Jacques Perrin, who produced and acted in it, used to go from one place to another trying to sell it; most of the actors and myself did the film for nothing. It was a very exciting time, but the major difficulty was trying to re-create Greece in Algeria. Not so much because of the architecture but the faces of the people.

Nobody expected the reaction it got, it was a surprise for everyone. The first week Z was in Paris nobody went to see it, and then audiences began to go and it all came together all over the world. I prefer not to speak about the repercussions; some people say the film did much against the colonels, but that's really just speculation. Financially we didn't earn very much. Jacques Perrin sold the movie in Italy for fifty thousand dollars at the time, and then the distributors made one and a half million and the same for a lot of other countries. So the percentages we had were really very small indeed.

JP *The Confession* was an extraordinary film in several ways, wasn't it?

CG During the shooting of Z we were all very interested in what was going on in Czechoslovakia. I went back to Paris and during Christmas a friend of mine, Jean-Paul Sartre's secretary, told me about Artur London's book *The Confession*. I read it and knew this was a book that had to be made into a movie. I was actually in the cutting room of Z, reading about the oppression inside Czechoslovakia. People say right-wing or left-wing, I generally simplify and just think of oppression. To me the right has always meant people who are against freedom, people who are racist. When I was young they said Stalin was very left-wing, I always thought he was as right as Hitler and Franco – with some differences of course. I asked Yves Montand and Simone Signoret if they would do it; they agreed. It was a time of mixed-up philosophies because all three of us were thought of as being on the Left, which we were, but here we were opposing the pro-intervention line of the Communist Party.

The reaction to the film was very violent, very violent. At first it came from the Communist parties, then from some socialists because at this period they were trying to get together with the communists. Internationally, people who had never even seen the film reacted against it. There were articles written in the Soviet Union, Czechoslovakia and elsewhere against me and Yves Montand. They tried to separate myself and Jorge Semprun who wrote the script from Yves and Simone, trying to say that they just followed us without really understanding. The most extraordinary thing is that four or five years later the Communist Party took the opposite position, the movie was shown on television and during a discussion afterwards a high-ranking member of the party said this was an important movie, the communists should be producing this kind of film. The line had changed, but the fight and the truth remained the same.

There was another extraordinary moment. A Chilean director whom I didn't know called me from Chile and said that they were using *The Confession* against Allende, saying that he had prohibited it. So I called Paramount in New York, they had the rights to it in Latin America, and they said it was just that it was summertime and they were waiting until the winter to show it. I got on a plane to Chile, spent all week going round and finding out what was happening, and then asked a journalist friend if I could meet Mr Allende. He said it would be OK. We had breakfast and we agreed to secretly record a television declaration. When it went out the next day it was kind of a bomb, nobody was ready for it. You see the attacks were trying to associate Allende with Stalin, my film was meant to show the threat to democracy that he posed. One day I was a good guy, the next a bad one. It was a sad time.

JP Did you enjoy making *Missing*?

CG Yes, yes because of the good conditions and particularly because of Jack Lemmon and Sissy Spacek who were with me all the way. They used to make jokes about my English, Jack still imitates my English. He plays the part of a man who remains a conservative, remains an American but changes his feelings first about his son, then about his perception of things and then about his country and its relationships with other countries. That was important, it would have been too easy to have that character changing from a conservative to a left-wing fighter; he always believed in the American quality of life and democracy and so forth. Jack Lemmon isn't kind of left-wing, he's a liberal who also believes in the ideas of America and he said, 'Thank God we have a country in which we can made movies like this.' So Jack and the character he was playing were similar, that helped a great deal. The film resulted in a law-suit against Universal for one hundred and fifty million dollars; I'm afraid I'm not allowed to talk about that at the moment.

JP You've said that politics is a mixture of people and power. Could you elaborate on that?

CG I think that politicians in the small countries at least are a little bit like the dolls in a puppet theatre; someone dictates the movements for them. The super-powers decide our lives, the politicians are the intermediaries. But my own political beliefs are difficult to explain, they've more to do with ethics than politics. I believe that everybody must be free, live in a free country, everybody should respect other people's dignity and we should all have an equal chance in society. Now a lot of people say all these things, but there's a huge gap between words and acts and I never follow any leader in a religious way. When I have to vote for a parliament or a president I try to find the man who is closest to my ideas; it may change from one time to the next. The problem is that journalists and other people prefer to have a catalogue saying he's a communist, he's a socialist, he's a royalist and so on. It gives them a very clear line of thinking but it's not correct; society needs leaders and their politics to make the country go on, but they're just hired for the job, if they don't do it well then throw them out.

Political violence has been going on since the Greek philosophers, since the Christ and I think it'll take maybe ten centuries for that to change. It can be justified, in Greece during the war we resisted the Germans; today we talk of terrorism, but one word can't really deal with it. If you had some form of terrorism in Poland or Czechoslovakia everybody would say bravo, go on and continue. But when you have it in Guatemala, which is even worse to live in, people are not so enthusiastic. You cannot justify terrorism in a free country like Italy which has free parties, free press, free unions, free everything – there is no reason to act through violence, there are other ways of expressing yourself. We have to examine the situation before we condone it or not, before we call someone a terrorist or a freedom fighter.

JP Has a film any real power to change a situation?

CG Oh I don't think so. And it's better that way, because if a movie could change things everybody would use it in politics, life, everywhere. Fortunately it cannot happen. A movie can add a small piece on a general movement or a general feeling but that's all. Propaganda exists of course, it was used by the Nazis and it's used now. I was dining with Lilian Gish in Paris and she told me that when she was young she came to Europe with her mother to make a movie, propaganda to convince the American public that the United States should come into the war. Audiences are less naive now. I remember going to see *Missing* in New York and they'd have discussions during the movie about whether it was true or not. I don't believe any one man can make a propaganda film. *Z* and *Missing* weren't propaganda films at all, they weren't linked to a system or a political party. It's one thing to express ideas and philosophy in a movie, quite another to be given money by a state to direct in a certain way. Of course, everything at one level is propaganda, even *Love Story* was propaganda for love.

JP You turned down opportunities to work in Hollywood, why was that?

CG First of all it would have been difficult because I'd already gone from Greece to Paris, going from Paris to Hollywood would have been very hard. To do a movie about America would have meant me going to live there for a year or two, I couldn't have done it otherwise. Then came the chance to make *The Godfather*. I turned it down because it was a little bit too pro-Mafia, it didn't speak about the connection between drugs and organized crime. I told the producers that if we spoke about the drugs trade I'd consider it, they just refused. Coppola did an extraordinary job, I'm not sure I could have made so good a movie. As to the money involved, it's important to be rich enough to be independent but that's all. I must tell you the best thing about the incident: I was speaking at a university in Boston and I mentioned why I turned the film down, seven or eight hundred people started to applaud.

JP There are a lot of films which never take hold of a subject, do you think directors have let us down?

CG If they all tried to make political movies it would be a very boring world; it's the same with books, newspapers and paintings. It's very hard to discuss it without being critical of other directors and that wouldn't be good. Conditions aren't easy for everybody, I was lucky with one or two big successes so I have all the freedom I need – I don't know if I'll have a film tomorrow but for the moment it's OK. Other directors are offered much easier movies, just simple love stories and thrillers or action films. It's important for a man to live and survive, and for a director to make movies. I don't want to become pretentious; it's very easy to tell other people what they should do. Things are never simple. It's a terrible thing to spend a year on a script and then have people with money say 'No' time and time again. So instead directors prefer to make a movie with perhaps less important philosophical content, but at least one that will be made. It's a question of balance and necessity.

I've taken some of the violence out of my films in the past. With the Greek colonels in *Z*, for example, they did much worse things, said much more ugly things, but we couldn't show it because it was just too incredible. There are something like fifty-six countries where more than 5,000 people are assassinated every year, it's worse than the Middle Ages. Cinema has a big responsibility here, it can cause familiarization with violence and that's an awful thing. For commercial reasons violence is brought into movies, which means that when people see real violence on the news they believe those people who've been shot will just get up after the cameras have gone. It's a vicious circle created by the Hollywood movie. I didn't show any real violence in *Missing*, I just tried to create an impression, people had to feel and imagine.

JP One gets the impression that you're not a typical European director, certainly your views aren't typical.

CG I come from a mass audience, I don't come from an elite so my films aren't for an elite. I feel much closer to what you might call the masses, the average people. I believe a movie must be exciting and fun as well as passionate. I only discovered the French life when I was nineteen so I had a completely different eye, I was something of an outsider. Sometimes I feel a bit like a savage coming to civilization. So I don't for example criticize television, I believe it enables people in small towns and villages who wouldn't go to the cinema to see movies; and I don't criticize musicals, in fact I'd love to make a musical, although it'd probably be a political one. For me the director is a person who can look at life and events with the possibility of almost starting again, he can participate in some way, like being in a meeting with friends he can discuss ideas and feelings. I like to think my movies can do that.

9 Patsy Spybey

Patsy Spybey is a very attractive young woman who was told, after a series of painful and often damaging operations, that she was suffering from an incurable disease and the rest of her life would be both short and hopeless. She rejected the overwhelming conventional wisdom of her doctors, searched and found an alternative cure to her affliction and is now recovering in her own way.

Not content to save herself, she worked with her husband Peter, a former nurse who is her constant companion and adviser, to organize an information service and aid group for others with incurable diseases. She is a lady of almost inconceivable courage and determination, having to fight not only her 'incurable' illness but also the apathy and discrimination of the community at large against the disabled.

She is a Birmingham woman of Irish origin, born in 1952. The national background is relevant because the disease could be traced plausibly to the nineteenth-century Irish famine. After differing diagnoses, including a stomach disorder and bone problems, the former model was finally told that she had Friedreich's Ataxia. Friedreich's is a wasting disease like multiple sclerosis. Unlike multiple sclerosis, however, there is no 'time off', only a steady and agonizing decline.

Patsy and her husband found a possible source of help in Germany with Dr Franz Schmidt, a medical professor at Heidelberg University. The couple saved and made the journey. Dr Schmidt immediately began a course of 'whole-cell therapy', consisting of injections of the cells of animal glands which have a revitalizing effect. He also changed her diet completely, allowing only natural and pure foods.

The changes are obvious. Able to take tentative steps for the first time in years, she is now active and optimistic. But the treatment is not scientifically proven in this country and Patsy has had difficulties with other doctors. 'Of course I cannot promise or guarantee anything', says Dr Schmidt, 'but I have fifty cases in my care, mostly handicapped children, and the treatment has had only positive results. Imagine what this means to a young woman like Patsy. The point is that for her and many others nothing is ever as hopeless as some would have us believe.'

The treatments in Germany cost £350 each and Patsy goes with Peter to have them twice a year. She gets a pension of £60 a week and he gets £16 a week dole money. He has sold most of his record collection and she has pawned her treasured possessions. On the last trip they persuaded British Airways to give them one free ticket, but they are currently £600 in debt. They are undeterred and on their last trip took a twenty-month-old baby with them, a Friedreich's Ataxia sufferer whose parents are among the many who have written to them in desperation for advice.

Patsy Spybey is an example of courage and an inspiration to many in this country. There is often a smile on her face, but underneath is a determination to persuade doctors in Britain to widen the research into her disease and the treatment of it. Her message is quite simple; it is one of hope.

JP   Patsy, when and how did you first realize that you were disabled?

PS   Really not until I was diagnosed which took about three or four years and to me that was the worst part. First of all the orthopaedic doctor told my parents that it was an orthopaedic problem and to have that put right I had my feet and legs broken, but after I had that done it was no better. I started being clumsy and bumping into things and losing my balance. Nobody suggested that I might have Friedreich's Ataxia, and when I was fourteen I was sent to a psychiatrist. At this stage I thought I was barmy; well you do at that age if you go to see a psychiatrist. After a couple of consultations he told my parents and myself that I was wasting his time. So then he sent me to see a neurologist and they diagnosed multiple sclerosis. At this stage I didn't know what multiple sclerosis was but something in me just said that I hadn't got it. I asked for a second opinion, they made me an in-patient and did a lot of clinical tests, and then said I'd got Friedreich's.

That period was from thirteen to sixteen and what made it bad was that even though I had something physically wrong with me I could never tell people what it was. If I went into a shop and my speech was a bit funny or I bumped into somebody their natural reaction would be, 'Oh, she's been on the bottle.' And I mean at sixteen years of age to be an alcoholic is terrible. What made it worse was that I couldn't turn round to anybody and say it wasn't a drink problem it was so and so, because I didn't know what was wrong with me. And even when I did find out that I had Friedreich's Ataxia I couldn't spell it, couldn't even say it!

JP   Now what is Friedreich's, can you describe it? And what was the progression of the disease through your teens?

PS   It's a disease that attacks the nervous system, there are no remissions or good periods, you just slowly go downhill. I can remember the doctor's words to this day. He said, 'You've got Friedreich's Ataxia, you can come and see me every year if you like but you're wasting my time and I'm wasting yours. I've got no treatment to offer you.' My balance was just loco, stupid really, but I was able to work until some doctor told my parents I had got a circulation problem and if they operated on my stomach it would help my balance and my blood circulation. We were guided by the doctor, I gave up work and had the operation and never really recovered from it. It was that which speeded up my Ataxia and gradually, by about twenty-one, I couldn't walk a distance and was relying more and more on the wheelchair. I think all doctors in those days were experimenting and I just wish to God that I had never had any of these operations, especially on my feet. When they said they wanted to do another operation on the other side of my stomach I had had enough. I said, 'Forget it, leave me be.'

I remember noticing the different way people treated me, as if I was a child. Because I was in a wheelchair they forgot that I was a woman with the needs and wants of a normal woman and they talked down to me. If I ever went out shopping with my husband I might ask for something but they'd never ask me for the money, they assumed I had no control over money just because I was disabled. Occasionally, if I was in a bad mood, I became angry but nine times out of ten I could laugh it off. I do remember when we went to buy a fridge and Peter was paying for it and arranging delivery and I was looking round the showroom at all the other things that were out of my price range. Someone came up and asked me what Santa Claus had bought me for Christmas and I must admit that I voiced anger very loudly. Peter became embarrassed and the person involved just walked away.

JP   Tell me how you met Peter?

PS   It was my second time in the nursing home and the place was buzzing that they'd got three male staff. I hadn't met them yet but part of my illness is where I'm desperate for the toilet first thing in the morning, and to get from the bed to the chair and along to the loo took too long, so they gave me a bedpan. One morning I used the bedpan, rang the bell and Peter appeared. It was the first time we met, not very romantic really. The courting had to be done very discreetly because we both knew that members of staff and patients aren't meant to. I used to tell the home I was going to church on a Sunday, Peter would take me, and that was our main courting day. We kept it secret for a couple of months but it was getting to me. Peter went to see the Principal who was very understanding and co-operative but warned him of the problems and that I hadn't got a long life-span, I suppose in her own way tried to put him off. Luckily it didn't work and we lived together for five years, then got married.

There's more pressure on the able-bodied person in the marriage, and a lot of people seem to think that we haven't got a sexual relationship, they skirt round the issue and won't ask questions. Sometimes they pity Peter, think that he's a normal man but he doesn't have a normal relationship with a woman and hasn't any freedom. They forget that when two people are involved it works both ways, and our relationship is no different from that of able-bodied people except that he has to do a lot for me. We still row, still argue. Still have good times and bad times. In a lot of ways my disability and campaigning has brought us closer together. We can laugh about my illness, as an outsider wouldn't laugh, and at some of the situations we have to. For example, nine times out of ten a women's disabled loo is inside a ladies' toilet which means Peter has to take me in. Sometimes women think we're up to hanky-panky and don't like it. Or people will be too helpful and everything goes wrong. Like if Peter's taking me up a flight of stairs in a wheelchair you'll get someone who's very attentive and wants to help, and everything he touches on the wheelchair will fall off, so Pete and I straight away collapse in a heap over each other and then the person gets embarrassed and thinks we're laughing at him. Well I mean we're not, we're laughing at the situation.

JP   Before the treatment, and before your marriage, the pressures of illness much have damaged your relationship.

PS   It tore us apart. I was so ill and felt so ill that I used to try and hide it from Peter, because the more he knew that I was suffering or in pain the more he worried. When I became very ill, in the hospital with kidney infections and bladder trouble and what have you, I tried to put a brave face on and told Peter there was nothing to worry about. I wasn't being truthful to him and I suppose in a way wasn't being truthful to myself. I thought I'd wake up and it would all go away and we'd live a normal daily life. But it got worse, I wasn't sharing my feelings and we began screaming and fighting with each other and just grew apart. And we split up for a period of ten months. We were in contact and he wanted to come back but was frightened to. So I gave him an ultimatum in the end – you either come back today or not at all. I didn't really think he would take it but he did, and we haven't looked back since. If Peter hadn't come back I knew in my own heart and mind that I would have got rid of my home and gone into a nursing home, I didn't feel strong enough, character-wise to live on my own much longer.

JP   Then in 1981 you went to Canada, during the Year of the Disabled, and that was the turning point wasn't it?

PS   Well we had personal friends out there, an airline company gave us free tickets and the social services in Birmingham did a fund-raising event for me to have money for the trip. We saw doctors, people with Freidreich's Ataxia and we did television and press interviews. Through a TV interview we met a German lady who was campaigning to make a treatment for Friedreich's more widely known, and she came and spoke to Peter and me. We came back and spent about six months checking out this doctor in Germany. Everybody was for the treatment, my own personal doctor said I had nothing to lose, but we didn't have the money. Peter sold his car, friends and social workers rallied round and got the money together and we could afford it. I was still a bit undecided because some people had warned me about it, said it was potentially dangerous, but I was so low mentally and physically that I thought that if I did die through the treatment I was only leaving Peter behind and he was big and able enough to pick himself up and start again.

There are three parts of the treatment. First is the cell implants which he puts into my hip every six months. These are glands from sheep injected into my body which the Ataxia is slowly destroying, and the treatment goes on for five years. Then there's a diet which is mainly good wholesome food with no white bread or red meat and nothing out of a can or a packet. And I have to do a lot of physiotherapy and swimming exercises which can be a struggle at times. The doctor, Professor Schmidt, sat us down and asked what we wanted out of the treatment. Well Pete and I said we'd be happy if he could arrest the disease, and the doctor said, 'When I've finished with you you will walk.' For someone to tell me that, I was astounded, speechless, couldn't believe it.

The improvement started in a matter of hours, I got warm legs and feet which Ataxia people just don't have because of the circulation problems. I panicked a bit, it was difficult to believe. Before the treatment I couldn't dust my own home for instance because my co-ordination was bad and nine times out of ten I'd knock ornaments over and wouldn't be able to pick them up. I didn't have the strength to wash up after a meal, couldn't iron or pick a drink off the table or use a knife and fork. If the phone went and Pete wasn't around I wouldn't pick it up in case it was a stranger on the other end, they wouldn't be able to understand a word I said to them. I certainly wouldn't have been able to talk like this in an interview. General health improved, you know, I didn't have any kidney or bladder infections, a cold no longer felt like flu. Ataxic people have bad heart problems but mine cleared up in about eight or nine months and I don't take any heart drugs any more.

For the first six months doctors in this country didn't want to know, because it was only my general health which had improved. But after my second treatment my speech and eyesight had improved, my co-ordination was getting better and there

112

were a lot of records proving all this. My heart specialist agreed that my health had certainly improved but he wasn't going to say it was cell therapy and wasn't going to say it wasn't. Same as my family GP, agreed that I was getting better but wasn't going to say either way if it was or wasn't cell therapy. The medical profession in this country are afraid to come forward and use a new treatment. Now I'm sure to this day they'll find a queue a mile long if they wanted to do a trial, people would clutch at it – just as I did. I know now that I'm not clutching, I've had the treatment.

JP   Now you began a campaign to inform people about the alternative cures which do exist. Could you explain about that?

PS   We started a group based in the Midlands to help families with people with Friedreich's, give them moral and mental support and hopefully to make doctors aware that there is this treatment being used abroad. When I was in hospital Peter was at home and had nothing to fill his days so he'd go to libraries, read about Friedreich's and come up against a brick wall. Also I was down because there was nothing to stimulate my brain. So we rang up the local radio station and asked for people with Friedreich's or with rare illnesses to get in touch. We were shocked by the response, we hadn't realized just how many rare illnesses there were. We co-ordinated it all together and literally plagued the press people to do some sort of story in the newspapers to make Friedreich's better known. I meet and see children with the illness and try to talk to their parents. It's difficult not to show emotion because these children are eight and nine years old; I had a normal childhood, they haven't. I try to show them understanding and give some tips but when I come away I often sit and have a good cry over it. Then the hurt goes and the anger gets in, and then the anger dies down and I think all that rolled into one gives me motivation to at least try and do something.

JP   Although it seems extraordinary, you have had opposition.

PS   Yes. People have said that I'm putting false hope in people's eyes. But to me everybody's got to have hope and encouragement, even if they aren't ill. I've had medical opposition, I've had press opposition, all sorts. The more I have the more determined I am to fight. And then there are the cranky calls. One guy in particular must spend a fortune in phone calls; he calls any time of the day or night and won't say anything, or sometimes he might laugh and get abusive. We never go to bed at night without taking the phone off the hook. I mean we've had calls at two, three in the morning. Someone's threatened to blow my legs off, said cripples should be put down at birth. Now I just think that the people who do these phone calls are to be pitied.

JP   How about when you rang up the *Sun* newspaper, could you tell that story?

PS   Well I phoned up because it was the Year of the Disabled and I suppose I was trying to prove to myself and to everybody that I was a normal woman with a normal figure like any other woman in the street. So I phoned up the *Sun* and asked them if I could be a page 3 girl. They took all my measurements, they were very interested and asked me to send a photo. After the interview I said, 'Oh by the way, I'm disabled and in a wheelchair.' The person on the other end of the phone said they weren't interested, it was immoral. Why is it immoral? I've got the same body, I said. Well I won't say what I said because it wasn't pleasant, but I came off the phone and I was very, very angry. To me that is discriminating against disabled people, a lot of people when they hear the word disabled they think you're grotesque. And I don't class myself as grotesque.

JP   What embodies hope to you now?

PS   Just to get better or to see my health improve and to be a proper housewife to my husband instead of him caring for me every day. Just the tables reversing. I don't strive for big things, I'm not a career woman. I just want to be a normal independent housewife, you know. If I want to go to the local shops for a loaf of bread or a pound of potatoes I'd like to be able to put on my coat and say, 'Right, I'm off.' That's all I'm looking for out of life.

10   Ken Livingstone

On an exhaust-stained wall in a borough of inner London is a sentence of graffiti. It reads 'I'd be willing to die for Ken Livingstone.' The sentiment is by no means unanimous; there are more than a few people who would prefer that Mr Livingstone's influence, at least, expired; but it demonstrates the extremes of emotion and feeling that the man has provoked in just three years in public office.

Ken Livingstone's accent is distinctly South London; he was born in Streatham in 1945 to a Scottish merchant seaman and former music-hall performer. He describes his parents as working-class Conservatives, but says his father was uncompromising in his anti-racialism. He failed his 11+, attended Tulse Hill school and gained four O levels. He admits to being something of a drop-out as a pupil.

It was an individual teacher who drew his attention to world affairs and focused his view on broadly political subjects. This was the period of Suez, the 'wasted years' of Tory rule, and Ken Livingstone's views came to fruition during the political upheavals of the 1960s. From then on, Livingstone's rise was both meteoric and mundane.

After gaining a teaching certificate at college and failing to obtain a job as a London Zoo keeper he worked as a laboratory assistant in a cancer-research institute. In 1968 he joined the Labour Party and three years later was elected a councillor to Lambeth Borough Council. In 1973 he was elected to the GLC and in the May of 1981 became leader of the Greater London Council after the Labour group had regained control.

Livingstone's period of leadership has been an era of modest reform, attempted major reform and media exposure. It coincides with the emergence of a new radicalism inside the Labour Party and of the maturing of a generation of younger socialist politicians. He has been the popular spokesman for this trend in London, and consequently has been the object of both acclaim and reaction. Moreover, he appears to have broken a mould, in so far as the perception of the man of government has been fundamentally altered.

With the exception of Tony Benn and Arthur Scargill, Ken Livingstone has been the target of more journalistic abuse than almost any other contemporary public figure. And it all seems the more intense because he appeared to materialize out of nowhere into political power. He, of course, would have been attacked merely for being a Labour leader. The fact that he has been *genuine* in his endeavours to bring tangible popular change, such as his attempts to introduce the 'Fare's Fair' proposals, has made him a love-to-hate bogey man. His support for the women's movement and for ethnic and homosexual groups has served to reinforce this image.

In December 1982 he reached his nadir of controversy when he invited Sinn Fein leaders to London and was frustrated by a Home Office decision banning them. He later met Sinn Fein MP Gerry Adams and in August 1983 said that what Britain had done to Ireland over 800 years was worse than Hitler's treatment of the Jews. He now says the remark was taken 'out of context' but it left some with the suspicion that he was perhaps as much a devotee of raw controversy as a radical politician seeking change.

He also has the rare ability to restore publicity to his advantage. Although the *Sun* described him as 'the most odious man in Britain' he has avoided much of the personal vitriol poured over other left-wing figures. For example, the *Standard*, long an opponent of Livingstone, has had to admit that its own surveys reveal a great deal of support for him from the most unexpected sources, including Tories.

At the time of writing, the Thatcher government is pushing ahead with its plans to abolish the Greater London Council. Ken Livingstone claims that he cannot think of 'a nicer job than leader of the GLC', but he also admits that he has parliamentary ambitions. If the Tories succeed in taking away his job and propelling him into national politics, they may have cause to regret their current campaign.

JP   What is so fascinating about you is that for years you've been working away in local government, but until you became leader of the GLC few had really heard of you.

KL   That's only because the British media don't study local government. If we were like the Americans with their interest in state and city politics you would have heard about me, but before I became leader if I was mentioned twice a year in the *Evening Standard* I was happy. Now there's this massive overkill, me being in the news every two minutes. It's an indication of just how poor coverage of local government has been, and that's not just the fault of the media, it's the fact that for years it's been marginalized. Not since Herbert Morrison used the old LCC as a base for the next Labour government has any really dramatic even happened in local government. It was seen as unattractive, a side issue, and if people wanted to achieve anything they went into parliament.

On another level is the whole issue of corruption. The scale of corruption is probably overrated in the big cities, because you've got so many people scrabbling up the greasy pole if they get the chance to stick the knife into anybody's back they'll do it; you tend to get corruption on the local councils when there's been a long period of one-party rule or one totally predominant figure as leader and all the rest deadheads. In places like Manchester, Birmingham and here that would be very difficult to get off the ground; you're never in that position. And there are less and less moribund boroughs. Views towards local government are also changing a little because more people on both sides of the House of Commons have a local-government background, and that just wasn't the case a few years ago.

JP   The point has been made, and in particular when you and your policies are discussed, that there is a sense of powerlessness around, that change isn't really possible. Is there, for example, a problem of being 'accepted' and maybe taking that acceptability too far?

KL   It isn't a question of absorbing revolutions, it's the point that individuals and characters have in the past been absorbed, ground down or bought off or whatever. We've never had a genuine mass movement which has been absorbed, it's been betrayed and sidetracked. The media got us wrong in the beginning, got their analysis of me completely wrong, now they take comfort in seeing the GLC as typical, lovable and eccentric British lefties. We were thought to be bed-sitter Trots; I've never seen a bed-sitter Trot, or for that matter a bed-sitter Stalinist. Now that the media see that they were wrong they're faced with either saying that radical socialists can achieve something in Britain, or calling us eccentric and noting the salamanders.

They go for the latter.

I'm not so sure that there is a danger of appearing too respectable or lovable; if Lenin had been able to appear on chat shows in 1905 perhaps he would have been able to take over a decade earlier, you don't know. Why is it that people expect politicians to be obnoxious and boring? Politics should attract the best and the brightest in each generation. It's a very British attitude to be so cynical towards politics, and especially left-wing politics. We've had socialist leaders from West Germany and the low countries over here and they can't understand what all the fuss is about, why we're seen as so extreme. I'd just be part of a pretty normal generation of left-wingers in Europe, here I'm seen as a dangerous revolutionary. The GLC isn't doing anything different from what a lot of German cities and some French towns are doing.

JP   How have you managed to make your form of socialism appear attractive to a wide range of people?

KL   You have in this country a mass of working-class Conservatives, my parents were, who are the people who enable Tory governments to be re-elected. These people have no real interest in being Tory but because of the way Labour is perceived and the inadequacy of Labour governments and the glow after Churchill they've never thought in any other way. Now in one sense our transport policy mainly benefited Tory voters, people coming in from outside the inner city. Men and women who'd never done anything but vote Conservative saw that they could benefit from a socialist Greater London Council.

But the entire question of my popularity or how acceptable our policies might be has been overstated. I was never as unpopular as they said, and I'm not as popular as I'm meant to be now. If you look objectively at the press coverage of us during the last three years, and that is all it is, it's complete madness. There's no way we could have rocketed between those two extremes. What has made matters easier for me and the GLC is that we can cut the fares, we can put on the marathon, we can put on Thames Day. Compare that to, say, Tony Benn or Arthur Scargill. Benn has consistently been kept away from any ministry where he could build up a popular base, and Scargill will inevitably come into conflict and can only be involved with the mines, although both of them are a lot more popular than we're told. If you look at the history of the British, I can't think of another group of radical left-wingers that have actually got hold of such a good instrument; we've been able to make ourselves more popular simply because of that. In a Labour government it would always be a fight to get policies past Wilson or Callaghan; people here actually have my encouragement. Imagine what a Labour government could do in five years if it operated in the way we have done.

It's also significant that from the moment we took over we've never overlooked the fact that we had to go out and campaign, explain what we were doing. In three years we've been able to get the building into a reasonable shape in terms of a PR machine. That's important, because there's a real choice on the Left about the terminology you use, you can turn people off so quickly without any effort. People just won't accept jargon, you've got to reduce socialist policies into terms of how it influences their everyday lives. and you've got to use the language they use. One of the problems on the Left is that it's over-academic, there are too many people who are full of verbiage. You have to communicate.

JP   Sean MacBride made the point that after he left the IRA and joined the establishment as a Foreign Minister his principles were eroded, power almost corrupted him. Looking at what you have said over the years, you seem less punchier now.

KL   Each new horrifying media experience educates you into how to say the same thing but not allow the media to distort it. Take for example what I said last year about the impact of Britain on Irish history; I could have constructed it in a way that would have made it impossible for it to be boiled down to a sentence of 'worse than Hitler' and so on. But at the time I wasn't thinking on those lines, and we saw what happened. Ronald Reagan actually said some years ago that the reason he won and Barry Goldwater didn't was that Goldwater would begin a speech by saying something shocking and then qualify it, but by that time everybody was reeling around on the floor. What Reagan does is to start with his soft, schmaltzy bit and gradually get round to saying the shocking thing. Very often now if I want to say something which I know can be misinterpreted I write an article in *Labour Herald*. I did that when I was opposed to the appointment of Sir Kenneth Newman. With a long article journalists haven't got any excuse if they twist what I've said.

On my particular statement that British treatment of the Irish is like what the Nazis did to the Jews, I said that for a quite simple reason: there is nothing else in modern history on that scale. It would have been no good drawing the analogy of the Turkish treament of the Kurds or the Armenians, or what we did to the Tasmanians when we hunted them to extinction – these things just aren't known; the only one that is perceived is what Hitler did to the Jews. I meant to say it, but you've also got to realize that, given that I make probably three speeches a day and have the media round me all the time, mistakes will happen, sometimes I'll say the wrong thing. A learning process has been at work over these three years, and one of the most important things which happened was when I was given a tape-recorder; I simply put it on the table during an interview or a press conference and you can actually see their faces change.

JP   Where does your socialism come from, and how do you fit it into a country which is so divided?

KL   I think you have cycles on a progressive scale, and we're in the bad part of a cycle at the moment just as we were in the 1930s. After that came the 1945 Labour victory and a radical government, just as in 1906 the Liberals changed things, and we're due for one now. It's always after a period of unrest and problems, and the difference this time must be that we take hold of the opportunities. Change in the political process influences every aspect of society. We nearly touched on something like that in the sixties with Pope John XXIII and the radicalism in the church, Kennedy coming after tired old Eisenhower, and we thought with Harold Wilson over here – horrifying. It got lost, ran into the Vietnam war, ran into incredible mismanagement of the British economy by a particularly incompetent Labour government, and all that has survived is the artistic side, the personal lifestyle aspect.

Next time we've got to make certain that we've learned the

lessons of the past, got to persuade people that a devolution in power is essential, got to merge style with where you stand in the political spectrum. So we wouldn't just be talking about economic change or welfare change but changes in power relationships between men and women, black people and white people. I don't believe you can achieve socialism while fifty per cent of society exploit the other fifty per cent, and this is something which men in Labour party don't really want to examine because they build their careers on the sacrifices of the women they live with; how can a radical transformation of society be brought about by a group of people who are exploiting the people they are supposed to love the most. You've got to start moving in these directions, and if you get it right there will be a permanent governing majority of the Left.

Feminism is crucial to all this. There are millions of women who've never considered voting Labour suddenly seeing that it's actually liberating their style of life and enabling them to do things they hadn't even dreamt of. If you look at the concessions that Neil Kinnock has made since he became party leader, they concern the demands that women have made for change in the party, whilst he's still tried to purge Militant and so on. That's probably got something to do with the influence of his wife who is a strong feminist although not plugged into the networks of radical feminism. You cannot exclude half of society and have a society worth living in. And feminism is the next really dramatic change, and perhaps one which will not be rolled back by a future right-wing government.

JP   But one point is still not clear. How *do* you deal with the 'corruption' of outsiders as soon as they become insiders?

KL   One of the things we've done here to prevent people just being bureaucratized is that I don't have any real contact with the bureaucracy. The pattern of Labour governments in the past has been the Prime Minister surrounded by key civil servants running the whole show, but we've devolved all that happens to the relevant committees and the committee chairs come to me when there's a problem. I had the Director-General in my office the day I became leader and told him I would not have any chief officer coming to me complaining about what members are doing; they take complaints to the member concerned. I meet the committee chairs and see the pressures which they're under and it's me who remains the radical force; that's the complete opposite of what usually happens. The party leadership must remain exactly that and not become enmeshed in the machinery of government, because every other poor sod is and the leader has to remind them of what they were elected to do. You're only corrupted if you come to be corrupted; you can be beaten or sidetracked, but that's a different thing.

JP Some of your supporters were concerned when you began to appear with opponents on chummy television chat shows as a 'celebrity'. Is that something you regret?

KL No. Not at all. It's a key issue because we've now got a request to do another series. Everybody around me, all the activists I consort with said that it was appalling and that I shouldn't have done it. But when you met people in the street they loved it; security guards or drivers would say 'I used to think you were a real nutter but I really changed my mind when I saw you in that setting.' Part of the problem with politicians is that they're not often in the settings that people can relate to. If they see you in that way, the next time you speak politically they listen to you. It's no good being pristine pure and having nobody listen to a word you're saying.

The Queen opening the Thames Barrier was a similar issue. We'd been getting indications for a long time that she wanted to do it, and with the threat of abolition from the government we needed to use that. And on the day I met her I bowed to her – again there was criticism. But if I hadn't the whole of the media, who just wanted a shot of me bowing to the Queen, would have screamed about 'Ken's snub to Queen', 'Royal Insult' and all of that. An emergency council meeting would have been called, there would have been a furore. It just wasn't worth it.

JP Do you enjoy the 'fame' of being Ken Livingstone, or do you find it a hindrance?

KL It's mixed. About once a year I get into a taxi and the man says 'No charge, a pleasure to take you,' and about once a year a taxi driver will slow down and say, 'I'm not taking you anywhere shit-head.' It varies. It could be nice to have a little bit less recognition. Most of the media coverage of my private life is absolute nonsense; sometime last November an old friend from my past who I hadn't seen for years turned up and said, 'What's all this about you being celibate?' This was the image projected, that my entire life had been sacrificed to sitting at this desk, that's rubbish. What I've done is to refuse to discuss my private life, and the media know that and stop asking. They don't need to know, and I don't want to use my relationships on a political basis. I do object to all these MPs who fill every election address with pictures of their wife and children, that's basically saying, 'Look I'm all right, I'm not gay.'

I'd prefer a bit more of a private life but the balance isn't too bad at the moment. Even at the height of the media hysteria about the GLC the journalists who were meant to be getting stories on me didn't do a very good job. They'd sit outside my flat for a while but that was about it. There was no real effort made to follow me and see where I was going, and they could have done if they'd put their minds to it. Occasionally I see that the rubbish in my dustbins has been gone through – great investigative journalism, a large pair of rubber gloves. It's ironic, but I've probably benefited from the poor calibre of the press in this country; that's one aspect of the media I suppose I shouldn't complain about.